Praise for *Strength for the Cancer Journey*

No one wants to hear the word *cancer*. I was not prepared for it—the uncertainty, the depression. In *Strength for the Cancer Journey*, Debbie Barr weaves the reflections of other cancer patients with her God-centered perspective, giving us courage and hope to walk this journey with Christ.

Joe Lineberry
Winston-Salem, North Carolina
Seven-year prostate cancer survivor

Debbie Barr's writing provides biblically sound encouragement for anyone walking on or alongside someone on a journey with cancer. These devotionals help to provide perspective, comfort, and peace during a time that can be filled with uncertainty. It is a great reminder that God cares for us and is in control.

Josie Kost
Pittsburgh, Pennsylvania
Breast cancer

I'm a thirteen-year survivor of an incurable cancer, multiple myeloma. As a cancer patient and author, I have deeply appreciated this devotional by Debbie Barr. She normalizes the unique feelings we have when fighting our disease. At times, I could feel her walking alongside, reminding me I am not alone, others have been where I am . . . and more importantly, the Lord is with me.

Maggie Bruehl
Cru Staff Emeritus, Orlando, Florida
Thirteen-year multiple myeloma cancer survivor

Cancer stirs an interest in faith like no other disease in my experience. Debbie's book of devotions is comforting and uplifting in its choice of scriptures and anecdotes.

Laurie White
Greensboro, North Carolina
Non-Hodgkin's lymphoma

The common thread woven throughout each devotional that Debbie shared is that God is writing each one's story. The most exquisite work may not be completely revealed until one day when we recognize what He was accomplishing during those days that were the darkest. As you digest each devotional, may you better understand the depth of spiritual growth that comes from greater intimacy with Him.

Kenneth E. Gorton
McMurray, Pennsylvania
Liver and stage 4 bone cancer

Through this devotional Debbie has touched so many areas that need to be faced during the journey of fighting cancer! She weaves together God's heart and healing words of truth that address raw emotions and fears. I was blessed and encouraged as she reminds the reader to "Look Up!" to where our help comes from (Psalm 121:1–2).

Nancy M. Wilson
Orlando, Florida
Stage 4 ovarian cancer

STRENGTH
FOR THE CANCER JOURNEY

30 Days of Inspiration, Encouragement, and Comfort

DEBORAH BARR

MOODY PUBLISHERS

CHICAGO

All Scripture quotations, unless otherwise indicated, are taken from the *Holy Bible, New Living Translation*, copyright © 1996, 2004, 2007, 2015. Used by permission of Tyndale House Publishers, Inc., Wheaton, Illinois 60189, U.S.A. All rights reserved.

Scripture quotations marked NIV are taken from the Holy Bible, New International Version®, NIV®. Copyright © 1973, 1978, 1984, 2011 by Biblica, Inc.™ Used by permission of Zondervan. All rights reserved worldwide. www.zondervan.com. The "NIV" and "New International Version" are trademarks registered in the United States Patent and Trademark Office by Biblica, Inc.™

Scripture quotations marked ESV are from The Holy Bible, English Standard Version® (ESV®), copyright © 2001 by Crossway, a publishing ministry of Good News Publishers. Used by permission. All rights reserved.

Scripture quotations marked KJV are taken from the King James Version.

Scripture quotations marked AMP are taken from *The Amplified Bible*. Copyright © 1965, 1987 by The Zondervan Corporation. *The Amplified New Testament* copyright © 1958, 1987 by The Lockman Foundation. Used by permission.

Scripture quotations marked AMPC are taken from *The Amplified® Bible (AMPC)*, copyright © 1954, 1958, 1987 by The Lockman Foundation. Used by permission. www.Lockman.org.

Edited by Elizabeth Cody Newenhuyse
Interior design: Erik M. Peterson
Cover design: Kaylee Lockenour

Library of Congress Cataloging-in-Publication Data

Names: Barr, Deborah, author.
Title: Strength for the cancer journey : 30 days of inspiration,
   encouragement and comfort / Deborah Barr.
Description: Chicago : Moody Publishers, [2020] | Includes bibliographical
   references. | Summary: "Strength for the Cancer Journey provides daily
   reminders that God is an ever-present ally for anyone facing cancer.
   Cancer is a journey no one wants to take, but no one has to walk that
   road alone. This devotional helps patients engage deeply with God,
   gaining strength for their cancer journey"-- Provided by publisher.
Identifiers: LCCN 2020004629 (print) | LCCN 2020004630 (ebook) | ISBN
   9780802419545 (hardcover) | ISBN 9780802498175 (ebook)
Subjects: LCSH: Cancer--Patients--Prayers and devotions. |
   Cancer--Religious aspects--Christianity.
Classification: LCC BV4910.33 .B375 2020 (print) | LCC BV4910.33 (ebook)
   | DDC 242/.4--dc23
LC record available at https://lccn.loc.gov/2020004629
LC ebook record available at https://lccn.loc.gov/2020004630

Originally delivered by fleets of horse-drawn wagons, the affordable paperbacks from D. L. Moody's publishing house resourced the church and served everyday people. Now, after more than 125 years of publishing and ministry, Moody Publishers' mission remains the same—even if our delivery systems have changed a bit. For more information on other books (and resources) created from a biblical perspective, go to: www.moodypublishers.com or write to:

Moody Publishers
820 N. LaSalle Boulevard
Chicago, IL 60610

1 3 5 7 9 10 8 6 4 2

Printed in the United States of America

Dedication

*I could not have written this book without the help of the eight
people who so graciously shared wisdom, insights, and stories from
their own very personal experiences with cancer. This "panel of
experts" spoke candidly in one-on-one recorded interviews, emails,
and texts to offer generous encouragement and support to others
on the cancer journey. Each is a sincere follower of Christ dealing
courageously with his or her particular cancer.*

*It is my pleasure to gratefully dedicate this devotional book
to these eight wonderful people:*

Jonathan (ocular melanoma)
Melody (breast cancer)
Jeff (prostate cancer)
Sheryl (multiple myeloma)
Lee (bladder cancer)
Laura (Hodgkin's lymphoma)
Dwight (prostate cancer)
Keela (breast cancer)

With heartfelt thanks to each of you,

DEBBIE BARR
Winston-Salem, North Carolina

*With their permission, the real first names of this "panel of experts"
are used throughout the book, except where otherwise noted.*

Contents

Day 1

Strength for the Journey

Don't be afraid, for I am with you. Don't be discouraged, for I am your God. I will strengthen you and help you. I will hold you up with my victorious right hand.

ISAIAH 41:10

There's nothing easy about having cancer. For most people, cancer is a hard, reluctant journey through rugged, unfamiliar terrain. If you have cancer now, or have had it in the past, you will understand the comments of some whose stories appear in this book:

Keela

When they called me from the breast clinic to come in for my results, I was thinking, "You know what? If it was good news, they would tell me over the phone." As soon as we went back into the office, immediately they gave me the news and passed out the Kleenex. It was hard.

Dwight

There's not a day that I get eight hours of sleep in a row. For example, last night I didn't sleep very well. I woke up after a few hours of sleep, and I went back and slept again. And when I woke up, I didn't have much strength. And that has happened multiple times this week.

Sheryl

When you get tired, when you're on chemo, you get *tired*. And you can't buck up and just keep going. No, you can't. You've got to stop.

Jeff

When you work a plan out with your healthcare team and things don't turn out the way you anticipated, and they don't turn out the way that your team anticipated, it's really hard to deal with.

Laura

They said this is an easy cancer to cure, even though I feel like it's been a long, hard road.

The apostle Paul journeyed "a long, hard road" of a different sort. He wasn't thinking about cancer treatments when he, led by the Holy Spirit, penned these words about his personal affliction, which he described as "a thorn in my flesh":

> Three times I pleaded with the Lord to take it away from me. But he said to me, "My grace is sufficient for you, for my power is made perfect in weakness." Therefore I will boast all the more gladly about my weaknesses, so that Christ's power may rest on me. That is why, for Christ's sake, I delight in weaknesses, in insults, in hardships, in persecutions, in difficulties. For when I am weak, then I am strong
>
> (2 CORINTHIANS 12:7–10 NIV).

The Bible doesn't tell us exactly what Paul's "thorn" was. However, the Greek word that he chose as a metaphor for his problem gives us a hint. The word he chose was not used to describe something merely bothersome, such as a cactus thorn. It was a word used to describe something much bigger, more like a tent stake.[1] Thus, Paul would have compassionately understood, as God surely does, any tent stake–sized "thorns" you encounter on your cancer journey.

Where can you find strength on the "thorny" days when you are physically exhausted, emotionally weary, or spiritually wavering? You will find your strength where Paul found his: in the One whose grace is sufficient for you and whose power is made perfect in weakness. God has the power to make you strong because He is *El Shaddai,* which means "Giver of Strength" in Hebrew. When everything in our lives is going well, we feel strong and self-sufficient. When we have the world by the tail (or so we think), we tend to trust ourselves rather than God. Often, only when a tent stake–sized thorn reveals the truth of our weakness, do we allow *El Shaddai* to infuse us with His strength, bringing glory to Him, not to us. This is a great paradox of the Christian life: we are strongest when we are weak.

There are really only two ways to face cancer: in your own strength, or with the help and strength that God supplies. Let this devotional book remind you, day by day, that *El Shaddai* is your ever-present ally on the cancer journey. As you draw upon His limitless supply of strength, may the words of the prophet Habakkuk describe more and more His powerful presence in your life:

The Lord God is my Strength, my personal bravery, and my invincible army; He makes my feet like hinds' feet and will make me to walk [not to stand still in terror, but to walk] and make [spiritual] progress upon my high places [of trouble, suffering, or responsibility]!

(HABAKKUK 3:19 AMPC)

He gives power to the weak and strength
to the powerless.—ISAIAH 40:29

FOR REFLECTION OR DISCUSSION

How does the paradox that *we are strongest when we are weak* apply to your cancer journey?

My journal . . .

Day 2

Why, Lord?

"My thoughts are nothing like your thoughts," says the LORD.
"And my ways are far beyond anything you could imagine."
ISAIAH 55:8

You have cancer.

Whether you have been walking closely with the Lord or running hard on a path far away from Him, those words stop you in your tracks and then bring you to your knees. *Cancer*—could there be a more unwelcome, more truly loathsome intruder? You have, no doubt, recoiled at the thought of cancer and perhaps struggled numbly to comprehend what sort of storm may lie ahead. And maybe your heart has voiced a silent, sincere question to God: *why, Lord?*

When Laura was diagnosed with stage 2 Hodgkin's lymphoma, she not only wondered *why,* but also why *now?* Just 29 years old, Laura and her husband were still settling into their first home and celebrating the birth of their newborn son when Laura's diagnosis came. The diagnosis explained a lot of the discomfort that had begun late in her pregnancy—the constant, painful crick in her neck, the dry cough that would not go away, and the small, odd lump in her neck. But *cancer? Now?* Thrilled to be a first-time mom, Laura just wanted to enjoy her new baby. But the cancer growing in her neck and chest was demanding her attention, forcing her down an unknown road and spoiling so much of her joy.

She poured out her grief to God: "Why do I have to go through this now, when this should be one of the greatest times of my life, having a son and enjoying him and being a mom?"

For the next year, Laura would reluctantly divide her time between her son and the demands of cancer treatment. It began with four rounds of chemotherapy, followed by a PET scan, then eight more rounds of chemo. Over the next several months there were blood transfusions, more scans, countless needle sticks, more chemo, the wiping out of her immune system, and finally a stem cell transplant. It was a long, grueling road. She lost her hair and her energy. "I had days where I wanted to give up because I was just tired of everything," Laura said. At her lowest point she remembers thinking, "There's no hope. I'm not going to be able to see my son grow up." But then: "One day I thought, 'You know what? I've got this—God's got me! I'm going to be okay.' And so I powered through. I'm so glad that He showed me to never give up and that I have so much to live for."

Still the *why* question remains: *Why* did Laura go through all this?

On this side of heaven, we may never fully understand the wisdom behind the *why*. But there may be a clue in something Laura said. Looking back on her cancer journey, she observed, "I had faith before the cancer, but it is a whole lot stronger now." Her experience is a reminder about how faith works. Just as muscles only grow stronger if they are continually challenged to bear more weight, so it is with faith. We grow much more in our hard times than when everything is going our way. So often, we do not yearn for God until we are broken by a painful problem or a hard circumstance we cannot change. Knowing this about us, and because of His immense love for us, God may allow adversity into our lives so that we will either return to Him or go deeper with Him. Sometimes the adversity God uses is cancer, even though God hates disease as much as we do.[1]

It is a mysterious and hard-to-wrap-your-head-around truth that *sometimes God permits what He hates in order to accomplish what He loves.*[2] And it pains Him to do so. The Bible assures us, "He does not willingly and from His heart afflict or grieve the children of men."[3] In *The Message*, this same verse, Lamentations 3:33, reads, "He takes no pleasure in making life hard,

17

in throwing roadblocks in the way."

Never forget that you are God's beloved child. All of His plans for you are good.[4] Our impassioned *"why Lord?"* is simply a reflection of the fact that His thoughts and ways are not like ours. Sometimes He draws us to Himself in ways we would never choose. So turn toward Him, talk to Him about your cancer, and allow Him to accomplish all He desires to do in you, for you, and through you because of it.

> *I had faith before the cancer, but it is a whole lot stronger now.*
> —LAURA

FOR REFLECTION OR DISCUSSION

How do you feel about the idea that *sometimes God permits what He hates in order to accomplish what He loves?*

My journal . . .

Day 3

Waiting

I waited patiently for the LORD to help me, and he turned to me and heard my cry.

PSALM 40:1

Waiting . . . it's just part of the cancer journey. Waiting to see the doctor. Waiting for test results. Waiting for surgery. Waiting while a prescription is filled. Waiting for chemo or radiation to start, then waiting for it to end. Even after it does end, the waiting continues: waiting to see if the treatments worked, and then as the years go by, waiting in an always-in-the-back-of-your-mind sort of way for the slightest indication of the one thing no one ever wants: the return of cancer.

Waiting is not easy.

The need to wait for so many things can add to the emotional distress of cancer. At times, waiting itself becomes yet another form of suffering. Even secular wisdom, however, recognizes the invaluable fruit that ripens as we endure waiting: patience. Businessman Arnold H. Glasow famously observed, "The key to everything is patience. You get the chicken by hatching the egg, not by smashing it."[1]

Keela admitted she struggles with this. "Patience is not one of my strong suits," she said. Dwight knows exactly what she means. He said, "One of the things that I've always had trouble with is patience. And going through these cancer trials and tribulations has required much more patience than I've ever needed before."

Nearly a century ago, a sage Christian wrote, "Patience can be acquired only just through such trials as now seem unbearable."[2]

In our generation, this is still true: whenever we must endure "such trials as now seem unbearable," invisible spiritual growth is taking place. Contemporary blogger Cortni Marrazzo described this truth well when she wrote:

> When a seed is planted in the ground, there is quite a bit of time between the planting of the seed and when something actually pops through the ground. From the surface, it looks like nothing is happening for so long, but that's because the growth is happening underneath the surface.
>
> When you're waiting, you're growing, even if you can't yet see the evidence of it. In waiting seasons, you will grow in faith and dependence on God, especially when you can't make things go any faster . . . It's in

these times that you'll realize how much your life depends on God.

This is when your trust in Him and in His plan for your life is tested; and subsequently grown the most.[3]

Waiting is one of God's favorite tools for making us more like Jesus. Waiting is never a waste of time if you lean into God while you wait. Whenever you encounter circumstances that you cannot change or when you can't make something happen on your timetable, you can be sure of this: God is at work in your life. James 1:3–4 tells us, "For you know that when your faith is tested, your endurance has a chance to grow. So let it grow, for when your endurance is fully developed, you will be perfect and complete, needing nothing."

Cancer treatments sometimes last for months or even years, and it's easy to grow impatient while waiting. Having received treatments for more than a year now, Dwight said, "God has impressed upon me that 'This is *My* time that we're on. It's not your time.' I'm learning that if you will be patient long enough, and focus on the right things, that God solves your problems. It's all about just being patient."

*For since the world began no ear has heard
and no eye has seen a God like you, who works
for those who wait for him!*
—Isaiah 64:4

FOR REFLECTION OR DISCUSSION

Is God using waiting to produce patience in your life?

My journal . . .

Boundaries

The words of the wise keep them safe.
PROVERBS 14:3

There are many kinds of boundaries. The fence that keeps an angry dog in his own yard is a type of physical boundary. Your skin is a physical boundary too. It defines the limits of your body and distinguishes what is "you" from all that is "not you." Even though they are invisible, words such as *no* also draw a boundary line. Your personal boundaries define what you believe to be the reasonable and acceptable ways for others to treat you. They also define how you will respond when someone steps over those limits. All boundaries have one thing in common: they establish limits that protect us.

As a person living with cancer, you may need to establish some boundaries to protect yourself from well-meaning but insensitive people. Author Lynn Eib shared an experience that illustrates this well. She wrote, "People used to come up and tell me gruesome stories about their neighbor who had the same kind of cancer

I did and just 'wasted away' or their grandmother who was 'racked with pain.' I hated hearing these stories, but at first I tried to be polite and listen. Finally, I decided I could take it no longer, and when people started a cancer story, I would interrupt them, smile, and say, 'Does this story have a happy ending? Because if it doesn't, I don't want to hear it.' That reply really stopped people in their tracks, and I didn't have to listen to any more hopeless cancer stories."[1]

By clearly stating the kinds of stories she did not want to hear, Lynn set a protective boundary. While you are on the cancer journey, you too may not wish to hear stories or comments that:

- Hint that you have cancer because your faith is too weak
- Blame you for past choices that, in the speaker's opinion, caused or contributed to your cancer
- Erode your hope
- Subject you to discouraging or frightening cancer stories
- Belittle your faith in Christ

When the words of others are discouraging or hurtful to you, it's very important to take care of yourself emotionally and spiritually and, when necessary, to set boundaries. For example, you can choose to limit the amount of time you spend with negative or discouraging people. You can also give yourself permission to stop attending any support group that doesn't deliver on the promise of support. That is, you feel worse after the meeting than before you came. Sometimes you may need to speak up, as Lynn did, using your own words to create a boundary of protection for yourself. Whether you are responding to an insensitive comment from a person who genuinely cares about you and actually means well, or a comment from someone who is deliberately being unkind, let the wisdom of Solomon guide you: *a soft answer turns away wrath, but a harsh word stirs up anger.*[2]

When you respond with a soft answer rather than an angry rebuttal, it may not only prevent an argument, but may also stop the flow of discouraging comments that erode the peace of mind and confidence you need right now. For example, if someone makes an "I told you so" comment, faulting you for something cancer-related that you did or did not do, a two-part soft answer might look like this:

- Make eye contact and smile at the person.
- Then humbly and gently say something such as: "Thank you for sharing your thoughts with me. I'm

unable to change the past, but I'm trying now to do everything my doctor recommends, and I would appreciate your prayers."

*All boundaries have one thing in common:
they establish limits that protect us.*

FOR REFLECTION OR DISCUSSION

Are there any boundaries you need to set while on the cancer journey?

My journal . . .

Day 5

Jehovah-Raah

The LORD is my shepherd; I have all that I need.
PSALM 23:1

Each person on the "panel of experts" for this book has chosen to journey through cancer walking close to God. From this place of spiritual comfort, they find it hard to imagine what it would even be like to fight cancer without the help of God. Sheryl, for example, wondered aloud, "If a person doesn't have God, how do they cope from day to day?"

For many people, a cancer diagnosis is a spiritual turning point. Jonathan said, "I don't think anyone is going to get cancer and remain the same. Someone is either going to really turn from God or run to God, one of those two things. The choice I've made is to run to God and ask Him for forgiveness and for a second chance."

Jeff said, "Christian or not, the thing I would want to get across to a newly diagnosed person is *God loves you. God is not abandoning you.* If they were a non-Christian, my thing would be to try to get them to understand that, no matter what, God loves you. I might not get through to them then, but my hope would be that I've planted a seed that the storms of cancer will water. And later when someone else comes along, that seed will germinate."

Sheryl, Jonathan, and Jeff each face their own cancer secure in the knowledge that they are in the constant, tender care of Jehovah-Raah. Jehovah-Raah means "the Lord my Shepherd." It is sometimes translated "the Lord my Friend."

Jehovah-Raah is the name of God in the familiar first verse of Psalm 23, quoted at the top of today's reading. The first part of the name, *Jehovah,* is derived from a Hebrew word that means "the self-existent one" and it suggests the idea "to become known." This name points to the fact that God is continually revealing Himself to humankind and that He wants us to know Him. Throughout the Old Testament, *Jehovah* was combined with other words, such as *Raah,* to further illumine God's character.

Raah comes from a word that means "shepherd" or "companion." Since the psalmist, David, was a shepherd himself, he knew well the kind of guidance, protection, and care a flock required. He observed how *Jehovah-Raah* cared for His flock, the Hebrew people, and he recognized Him as the perfect Shepherd. Through the timeless words of the 23rd Psalm, David still speaks to us today, encouraging us to rest in the care of *Jehovah-Raah*, the perfect Shepherd.

In his Bible commentary, John Gill says that Psalm 23 does not describe Jehovah the Father, but rather Jehovah the Son, Jesus. He points readers to John 10:14, where Jesus says, "I am the good shepherd; I know my own sheep, and they know me." Gill's elaboration on the first verse of the psalm is especially comforting to those with cancer because, as he notes, this good shepherd is both omniscient (all-knowing) and omnipotent (all-powerful). He writes,

> *being omniscient, [this shepherd] knows all his sheep and their maladies, where to find them, what is their case, and what is to be done for them; and being omnipotent, he can do everything proper for them; and having all power in heaven and in earth, can protect, defend, and save them; and all the treasures of wisdom and knowledge being in him, he can guide and direct them in the best manner.*[1]

If you have been facing cancer without a Shepherd, you can now be safe in the care of Jehovah-Raah. He is Jesus, the good, omniscient, and omnipotent shepherd. When Jesus is your Shepherd, Psalm 23 is your story of resting in His care.

The LORD is my shepherd; I have all that I need. He lets me rest in green meadows; he leads me beside peaceful streams. He renews my strength. He guides me along right paths, bringing honor to his name. Even when I walk through the darkest valley, I will not be afraid, for you are close beside me. Your rod and your staff protect and comfort me.
—PSALM 23:1–4

FOR REFLECTION OR DISCUSSION

What do these words of Jesus mean to you: *I am the good shepherd; I know my own sheep, and they know me?*

My journal . . .

Day 6

Roots

*Let your roots grow down into him, and let your lives
be built on him. Then your faith will grow strong
in the truth you were taught.*

COLOSSIANS 2:7

I was struggling to pay for my nausea medicine,"
Melinda* said. "It had gone from $45 for a three-
month prescription to almost $500, and I had to refill
it." When she mentioned her dilemma to a friend, the
woman remarked cynically, "Well, *you said . . .* " repeat-
ing what Melinda believes about the power of prayer
and God's power to heal her. Then, spoken in a way that
implied *if your beliefs are really true,* she told Melinda,
"You don't need that nausea medicine."

Melinda said, "I thought it was very insensitive of her
to throw God in my face like that. She wasn't beside me
when I was throwing up and putting my head on a cold
toilet just to get a little bit of relief."

Ouch! Even the miseries of cancer are not off-limits
for some insensitive or unbelieving people who want

to disparage faith in God. Perhaps someone has even suggested to you that if God really cared about you, you wouldn't have cancer. (Ouch again!) Billy Graham once responded graciously to a similar notion:

> Someone asked me recently if I didn't think God was unfair, allowing me to have Parkinson's and other medical problems when I have tried to serve Him faithfully. I replied that I did not see it that way at all. Suffering is part of the human condition, and it comes to us all. The key is how we react to it, either turning away from God in anger and bitterness or growing closer to Him in trust and confidence.[1]

While you are coping with cancer, how can you protect your heart from thoughtless comments as well as the mean-spirited ones that are meant to shake your faith? The answer is *roots!* Robert Murray M'Cheyne, a wise nineteenth-century Scottish minister, said, "When God gives a promise, he always tries our faith. Just as the roots of trees take firmer hold when they are contending with the wind; so faith takes a firmer hold when it struggles with adverse appearances."[2]

M'Cheyne's observation about tree roots and wind is supported by modern science. In the Biosphere 2 experiment, scientists created a miniature version of the earth under a huge glass biodome. It was designed to provide perfect conditions for people, plants, and animals. The trees thrived in the Biosphere until they grew to a certain height, then they simply fell over. In one writer's words, "It baffled scientists until they realized they forgot to include the natural element of wind. Trees need wind to blow against them because it causes their root systems to grow deeper, which supports the tree as it grows taller."[3]

In terms of faith, the metaphor is clear: you are the "tree" and the difficult circumstances and imperfect people you encounter are the "wind" that will strengthen your spiritual roots—if you let it. Remember Billy Graham's caveat: "The key is how we react to it." The winds that pummel your life can either move you "away from God in anger and bitterness" or toward Him "in trust and confidence." You have a choice every time a harsh wind blows against you.

Remember, you don't have to stand alone in the wind! The Lord desires to walk with you through every storm you encounter, so reach out and take His hand. In His faithful, powerful grip, you need not fear the wind, no matter what sort of wind it is. Whenever a powerful wind blows against you, God's purpose is always the same: He wants to deepen the roots of your trust in Him.

With her heart open toward God, Melinda pondered

how to respond to the "wind" of the hurtful comment noted above. She said, "God helped me to understand and to pray for that person and not to take it personally. It was their bitterness toward God that they were projecting onto me."

* not her real name

Just as the roots of trees take firmer hold when they are contending with the wind, so faith takes a firmer hold when it struggles with adverse appearances.
—ROBERT MURRAY M'CHEYNE (1813–1843)

FOR REFLECTION OR DISCUSSION

What "winds" are blowing in your life right now? How can you ensure that they will strengthen, rather than weaken, your faith?

My journal . . .

Day 7

Roller Coaster

*Jesus Christ is [eternally changeless, always] the same
yesterday and today and forever.*
HEBREWS 13:8 AMP

Roller coasters . . . dare to board one and you're in for a fast ride in a small, open car that jostles wildly down a track full of tight turns, steep slopes, and sometimes loops, backward rushes, spirals, and even water splashes. Whether you love them or hate them, it's easy to understand why roller coasters are a pretty good metaphor for the cancer journey.

"I hate to use cliché phrases," Jonathan said, "but cancer is that 'emotional roller coaster.' And I can't imagine this ending anytime soon. This is a ride I'll be on."

Laura describes her experience in much the same way. She said, "It's just been a roller coaster, really, with emotions, not blaming God and then blaming God. But in the end, I know that He is the Great Physician, and He was my doctor the whole time."

Cancer is like a roller coaster ride because it can make

you feel that your life has spun wildly out of control. And once you're on board and the coaster is moving, you can't just exit the ride any time you want to! It's not uncommon to feel helpless or overwhelmed, especially when first diagnosed. According to the Canadian Cancer Society, it is normal to experience many emotions, including any or all of these, while coping with cancer: shock, fear, denial, anger, guilt, anxiety, stress, loneliness, sadness, depression—and, on the positive side, hope as well.[1] The National Cancer Institute says that it's normal to feel these emotions "whether you're currently in treatment" or "done with treatment."[2] In other words, having cancer sometimes means being a reluctant rider on the proverbial "emotional roller coaster."

Experienced "cancer coaster riders" suggest three things that may help you maintain emotional balance:

1. Focus on something other than cancer. Pour some of your time and energy into something you really enjoy, such as painting, crafts, woodworking, gardening, restoring an old car, making a website— whatever your "thing" is—to take your mind off of cancer. Let this therapeutic use of your talent also be a gift to the Lord: "Whatever you do, work at it with all your heart, as working for the Lord" (Colossians 3:23 NIV).

2. Keep a journal or blog online. Research studies have found that good things happen when a person puts their deepest feelings about cancer into writing. One study found that "a single, brief writing exercise is related to cancer patients' reports of improved quality of life."[3] Other studies have found "that expressive writing produces such benefits as reduced physical symptoms and pain awareness, fewer doctor visits, and improved immune function."[4] If you have never kept a journal before, you may have mixed feelings about journaling. To find out whether it is something you would enjoy, why not try journaling for a few days in the space provided at the end of this devotional and the ones that follow?

3. Learn. Most people feel more in control when they understand the facts about their disease and its treatments. Ask your doctor to explain the things you don't understand and ask him or her to suggest educational materials for you. The more you understand, the more informed your decisions and prayers for guidance will be.

Roller coasters are full of surprises. You never know what hairpin turn or steep drop could be coming next, but that's part of the fun. It's why you buy the ticket.

The cancer journey can be as unpredictable as any roller coaster ride, but that's *not* fun, and no one wants to buy a ticket. The wonderful comfort for you, dear Christ follower, is that you are never alone on the cancer coaster. No matter how unpredictable the journey may be, the Lord who holds you snug in the palm of His hand never changes. He is indeed "[eternally changeless, always] the same yesterday and today and forever." Jesus is rocksteady and with you all the way, no matter what twists or turns you may encounter on the path ahead.

> God has said, "I will never fail you.
> I will never abandon you."
> —Hebrews 13:5

FOR REFLECTION OR DISCUSSION

Does it comfort you to know that Jesus is with you on the cancer coaster?

My journal . . .

Day 8

Not on Bread Alone

Jesus answered, "It is written: 'Man shall not live on bread alone, but on every word that comes from the mouth of God.'"

MATTHEW 4:4 NIV

Melody and Lee, a married couple, are both cancer survivors. Melody has had breast cancer twice, the first time before she married Lee, and the second time about seven years into their marriage. More recently, Lee has had bladder cancer. As they have cared for each other throughout their on-again, off-again journey with cancer, their faith in God has grown stronger. Their best tip for coping with cancer day by day is, in Melody's words, "trust God incredibly."

But how do you learn to trust God like that?

Lee and Melody say that what has most helped them to deepen their trust in God is a "go-to" list of the Bible verses that have been most meaningful to them. Said Lee, "We've looked at those verses hundreds of times." "Countless times," Melody agreed.

Having verses in list format is a great help, Melody

said, because "You're going to feel sick. And on a lot of days, there's no way you're going to feel like opening your Bible and trying to find a passage. So you need to have God's promises right there at your fingertips so that you can read them over and over and just meditate on them. For me, that was really important. That was critical."

Melody's cancer treatments are ongoing, and to this day, she says, "I keep my verses all over the house. Because life is real. And you just need to be constantly reminded of all the promises that we have in Scripture." She encourages others with cancer to make their own list of verses and "put them on your nightstand; put them in your pocketbook; put them in your wallet."

Sheryl, who has multiple myeloma, said, "I enjoy going to my Bible study class, and my church has a women's Bible study that has daily scriptures to read and sometimes memory verses. So whether it's the class, or the women's study, or just reading the Bible myself, I'm always in the Bible."

Jeff, now in his fourth year with metastatic prostate cancer, said, "When I start my day with God, if I don't have my Bible, I read it on my phone. I'll do devotionals during the day too." After his prostate cancer diagnosis, Dwight "armed" his iPad by downloading various versions of the Bible and Bible commentaries. He said, "When I look at a verse, I look at it in multiple versions and I read the commentaries and compare them."

If you are a new believer, or not yet a Christ follower, you may wonder why these people think it is so important to read the Bible while fighting cancer. Their passion to bring the Scriptures into their sojourn with cancer may be best explained by what the Bible says about itself:

- **The Bible is unlike any other book:**
  "For the word of God is alive and powerful. It is sharper than the sharpest two-edged sword, cutting between soul and spirit, between joint and marrow. It exposes our innermost thoughts and desires" (Hebrews 4:12).

- **Its words are eternal:**
  "Heaven and earth will disappear, but my words will never disappear" (Jesus in Matthew 24:35).

- **In our battle against evil, it is our only offensive weapon:**
  "Take the sword of the Spirit, which is the word of God" (Ephesians 6:17).

- **It guides us:**
  "Your word is a lamp to guide my feet and a light for my path" (Psalm 119:105).

The verse, "Man shall not live on bread alone, but on every word that comes from the mouth of God," affirms that you are more than just your physical body. You are a spiritual being too. Thus, it's not enough to just respond to the physical impact of cancer. Cancer has touched you emotionally, spiritually, relationally, and in other ways. It makes sense then, in your fight with cancer, to extend your focus beyond your body, and do more than just feed "on bread alone." It's important to also feast upon "every word that comes from the mouth of God"—the words of the Bible. These God-breathed words will deeply nourish your soul and enable you to "trust God incredibly."

You need to have God's promises right there
at your fingertips so that you can read them over
and over and just meditate on them.
—MELODY

FOR REFLECTION OR DISCUSSION

In the Appendix at the end of this book, you will find a list of thirty verses to help you "trust God incredibly" as you continue on your cancer journey. If you wish, you can add other verses to this list in the space provided.

Alternatively, consider creating a personalized list of
"go-to" verses as Melody and Lee did.

My journal . . .

Lonely

*Turn to me and be gracious to me, for I am
lonely and afflicted.*
—David, PSALM 25:16 NIV

Being alone and being lonely are not the same thing. One can spend time alone, perhaps reading or bicycling or working around the house, and not feel a bit lonely. It's also possible to be surrounded by family members or in a crowd of friends at a party and feel lonely. Many people with cancer have both experiences: times when they just want to be alone and times when they need connection with others but feel the pain of loneliness.

For one woman, a "bad cancer day" is an I-want-to-be-alone day. She said, "It's a day when I don't even want to take a shower and get dressed. I don't want to eat good food. I want to eat nothing but junk. I don't want to see anyone and I don't want to do anything. Just leave me alone." She speculates that "because I cycle on and off of the chemo, it could be the chemo doing that to me." She added, "Fortunately, those days are not very often."

Others with cancer find that an emotional gulf sometimes lies between them and those who don't have the disease. One woman wrote, "Cancer is a lonely disease. . . . Cancer feels isolating and can be very hard during the moments when you just want to talk to someone who 'gets it.'"[1] Another wrote, "Today I am lonely. . . . I know I have my friends and my family who love me. They would do anything I needed them to do. All I need to do is ask. But, they really do not understand how alone someone with cancer can often be."[2]

The Canadian Cancer Society website points out that those with cancer are not the only ones who may feel lonely. It reminds patients that sometimes family members and caregivers feel lonely too:

> They can feel as though they've lost their best friend or that they have no one to talk to about what they're going through. They may feel overwhelmed by new responsibilities. They may feel like they don't have time to see friends or do activities they enjoy. They may also feel overlooked by the healthcare team or family members and friends, who tend to focus on the person with cancer.[3]

Thus, even the strongest and most loving of relationships may be challenged by cancer, and everyone in a cancer patient's circle of relationships may be vulnerable to loneliness.

When you are brought low by the feeling that no one really understands what you are going through, remember that there is One who does. Your Lord *perfectly* understands how you feel, not only because He is God, but because He too has felt the pain of loneliness. On the most difficult night of His earthly life, Jesus' closest friends did not comprehend what He was facing or feeling. Though He told them He was overwhelmed with sorrow, they nodded off to sleep while He prayed alone. The Bible tells us, "And being in agony [of mind], He prayed [all the] more earnestly and intently, and His sweat became like great clots of blood dropping down upon the ground. And when he got up from prayer, He came to the disciples and found them sleeping from grief."[4] While He was still speaking to them, His betrayer, His own disciple, Judas, arrived with soldiers and guards carrying "lanterns and torches and weapons."[5]

Could there be a more lonely moment in all of human history?

When cancer feels like a lonely road to you, you can be sure that your loneliness is compassionately understood by the Lord. He hears when your heart cries out, as David's did, "Turn to me and be gracious to me, for I am lonely and afflicted." Though you may sometimes feel the ache of loneliness, you are never alone on the cancer journey. Jesus has promised to be with you every step of the way. His promise to you, as expressed in the Amplified Bible, is: "I am with you always [remaining with you perpetually—regardless of circumstance, and on every occasion] . . ."[6]

When you are brought low by the feeling that no one really understands what you are going through, remember that there is One who does.

FOR REFLECTION OR DISCUSSION

Is it difficult or easy for you to invite Jesus into the loneliness of your cancer journey?

My journal . . .

Support

If you really fulfill the royal law according to the Scripture, "You shall love your neighbor as yourself," you are doing well.
JAMES 2:8 ESV

Each person interviewed for this book expressed appreciation for the people walking the cancer journey along with them. The encouragement, kindnesses, and practical help of their loved ones, friends, church family, and others have helped them persevere. Jonathan said, "I have a very loving and supportive family; my wife and boys are great. My church is fantastic." Keela noted, "Even your nurse navigators are so wonderful, and they truly care."

Yet, unless they have had cancer themselves, even those providing such love and support cannot really understand what cancer patients go through. Jonathan explained, "You're dealing with something that could potentially be life-ending. And only people who are going through it can truly relate to that. That's why some type of cancer ministry, a support group or something, is beneficial—because we're the club that nobody wants to be a member of. And no one else can really understand what we're going through."

Members of the "club" often find a depth of camaraderie and understanding in a cancer support group that cannot be found elsewhere. In a cancer support group, everybody "gets it" because everybody is walking a similar path. Sheryl said, "I recently found a multiple myeloma support group locally. It's just fantastic to have that support group! We all share: *will I get help here? Have you talked to so-and-so? There's this new study going on . . .* There were five or six other people there that have multiple myeloma, and some caregivers too. It's just great."

Jonathan found support online from others with his same rare cancer. He said, "I knew that I needed to join up with some other people. So I joined Facebook and I'm a member of some closed groups. These people are supportive like you can't even imagine." Jeff also found support online. He said, "I felt like God was leading me to be open about my journey. If I had not gone public like I did on Facebook I would have withdrawn and I wouldn't have gotten the support that I have. Talking to people on Facebook gave me that boldness to talk to people at the cancer centers. If I hadn't gone that direction, I would have had a lot rougher road."

Melody says there's only one thing that's better than having a cancer support group: having a cancer support group *and* a group of praying friends. "There's just no substitute for Christian friends. Everybody needs to get a group like that." She urges, "Don't do cancer on your own! Let friends who are truly supportive and loving and who will pray for you know what's going on."

Surprisingly, some people need the most support *after* their cancer treatments end. Melody said, "It may sound crazy, but I've had friends who soared through chemo and radiation and crashed when it finished." Sometimes the "crash" occurs because when treatments end, support seems to end too. Post-treatment, people no longer have as much contact with their medical team. Their friends and family may think everything is now back to normal, and pull away a bit, leaving the cancer survivor now feeling that they are on their own.

By God's design, people are wired for connection with others, and we all need to both give and receive support. Paul tells believers, "Rejoice with those who rejoice, weep with those who weep" (Romans 12:15 ESV). Commenting on this verse, Dr. Charles Stanley wrote, "Both rejoicing and weeping imply genuine, heartfelt emotion. This kind of keenly felt connection happens only when we choose to get deeply involved in the lives of other believers."[1]

God wants you to both receive genuine support and also give it to others on the cancer journey. If you need a support group, prayer partners, or both, reach out! The American Cancer Society* can help you find a support group. Your local hospital may also offer cancer support groups. If you would like prayer partners, but Christian friends are in short supply, contact a Bible-believing church and make an appointment with a pastor or counselor there. He or she can connect you with people who would love to pray for you.

Don't do cancer on your own!
—*MELODY*

FOR REFLECTION OR DISCUSSION

What type of support do you need at this point in your cancer journey? What type of support are you able to extend to others?

* American Cancer Society Helpline: 800-227-2345; website: www.cancer.org

My journal . . .

Day 11

Promoters and Protectors

*Fix your thoughts on what is true, and honorable, and right,
and pure, and lovely, and admirable. Think about things that
are excellent and worthy of praise.*

PHILIPPIANS 4:8

Julie Lanford, "The Cancer Dietitian" at Cancer Services in Winston-Salem, North Carolina, writes a blog about nutrition and cancer. Two of her very helpful posts are titled "Eat More of These 'Protector' Foods" and "Eat Less of These 'Promoter' Foods." Protector foods, she explains, are "the foods that provide your body with the nourishment it needs to function at its best." Promoter foods are the ones "that do the opposite, and break down our body's ability to protect us against disease."*

What is true in the physical realm often applies in the spiritual realm as well, and that is the case here. Just as the foods we put into our bodies can either help promote disease or help protect us from it, what we put into our minds can either strengthen or weaken our outlook

* *Check out Julie Lanford's blog and recipes at cancerdietitian.com*

when we are face-to-face with an illness such as cancer. While you are fighting cancer, it is important to evaluate how the news media, the internet, your entertainment choices, and the people in your life all contribute to either a positive, empowered outlook or a negative, despairing one.

Author Margaret Feinberg can attest to the impact of negative comments from others. In an interview, she recalled that during her treatment for breast cancer: "Many people were supportive and prayerful, but then there were those who filled our inboxes with unsolicited medical advice, stories of everyone they knew who had died from cancer, retribution theology and accusations that I had brought the cancer on myself because of a hidden sin or lack of faith. Those kinds of comments are devastating when you're in the fight of your life."[1]

Laura's experience was the opposite, attesting to the positive impact others can have. She said, "All the positivity from people really helped me. People told me, 'You're so strong. You've got this.' Honestly, I need to hear the positive stuff. I cannot tell you one negative thing that somebody has said. It's all been positive." She said that even "random people," seeing that she had no hair, "have come up to me and said, 'Whatever you're going through, I just want to pray for you.'"

Dwight also believes that a positive outlook is essential.

He explained, "It's easier to fight things with a positive mental attitude than it is with a negative one. You find the positive and you continue moving in that direction. Because if you look towards the negative, you're only going to make it more difficult on yourself." Laura agrees. She said, "I've had my dark days. But I've had more positive days just because, I believe, a lot of it's in your head. I think that staying positive has really helped me the most, and leaning on God, knowing that He was going to get me through this."

Most everyone who is fighting cancer needs a bit of help to stay positive. Here's a checklist of spiritual "protector foods" that can help you sustain a positive outlook throughout your cancer journey:

- Reading and meditating on some part of God's Word every day
- Committing to memory the Scriptures that encourage you most
- Praying about everything that concerns you, remembering that nothing is too big or too small to take to God in prayer
- Talking openly with trusted others about your concerns and feelings
- Listening to uplifting Christian music
- Singing to the Lord

- Limiting your exposure to negative people and influences. This means being selective about what you open your "ear gate" and "eye gate" to admit. Stay mindful that the movies and TV shows you watch, what you read, the music you listen to, and the attitudes and words of others can either be "protectors" that lift you up with encouragement and hope, or "promoters" that bring you down with discouragement and fear.

You will keep in perfect peace all who trust in you,
all whose thoughts are fixed on you!
—ISAIAH 26:3

FOR REFLECTION OR DISCUSSION

Can you identify the "protector" and "promoter" influences in your life?

My journal . . .

Anger

*This change of plans greatly upset Jonah,
and he became very angry.*

JONAH 4:1

The biopsy results were back, and the news wasn't good. Seven of the twelve biopsy samples contained cancer cells. Jeff heard the doctor say "prostate cancer" but he didn't let the words sink in. He recalled, "I went in to work and I just stuffed it."

"That night," he said, "I was really angry. I mean, I didn't even pray."

That angry decision not to talk to God was more significant than you might guess. Here's the back story:

"I got sober in 1992," Jeff said. Back then, Jeff the recovering addict/alcoholic was not yet a Christ follower and he felt he had a very good reason not to pray. He told his Alcoholics Anonymous sponsor, "I don't like to get on my knees." The wise AA sponsor responded, "Throw your shoes under your bed."

"So for twenty-seven years," said Jeff, "I've kept my

shoes under my bed." He explained, "I've got to get on my knees to get my shoes when I get up. That reminds me to pray to God."

But on the night of his prostate cancer diagnosis, for the first time in twenty-seven years, Jeff did not put his shoes under his bed. He admits, "That night I was rebellious. I intentionally left my shoes downstairs." He continued, "So that next morning when I got up, I went to get my shoes and it hit me! I said, 'Oh, my Lord.' And I prayed. And I told Him I was mad."

It's not uncommon to feel anger, as Jeff did, upon receiving a diagnosis of cancer. Anger can also occur when a loved one faces cancer. When Lee's wife was diagnosed with breast cancer for the second time in seven years, he became angry. He said, "I was just angry that she had to deal with cancer again and was going to be subjected to yet another major surgery. It just didn't seem fair." He reflected, "I would understand anybody's anger with God. I expect a lot of people feel like they've been deserted by God. They're angry at God and they get further away from God instead of closer. I think that's a huge mistake. I think you just have to force yourself to stay close to God—daily Bible reading, anything you can do to remind yourself that God is there and will help you."

As time goes on, like Jonah in the verse above, many people living with cancer also become angry about the "change in plans" imposed on them by cancer. The losses and hardships created by the disease and its treatments can trigger not only anger, but any of the other now well-known stages of grief (denial, anger, bargaining, depression, and acceptance). Though much of the general public is now aware of the grief cycle, what many people don't know is that these stages were not originally developed to help people grieve the loss of a loved one, but to describe what *patients* go through in coming to terms with a potentially life-threatening disease such as cancer.[1] It's important to know that the five stages do not occur in lock-step linear order, but unpredictably, in any order at any time: a messy process.

Whenever you experience cancer-related anger—perhaps toward cancer itself, the healthcare system, your healthy friends or family members, or, like Jeff, toward God—*it's okay!* Anger is neither right or wrong; it's just a feeling. (What you *do* with your anger, however, *can* be right or wrong, so be careful not to take your anger out on other people. Instead, express your anger in non-destructive ways: punch a pillow, yell when you are alone in the car, clean the house, or hammer a few nails, for example.)

Sometimes anger comes from other deeper feelings that are more difficult to express, such as fear, anxiety, or helplessness. That's one reason it's wise and emotionally healthy to talk about anger instead of holding it in. When you are comfortable doing so, talk about your anger with a counselor, a close friend, or in a cancer support group. And, of course, you can always be completely transparent with God, even if He's the one you're mad at. Remember, God is the author of all human emotions. If anyone understands your anger, it's God! So don't hold back—tell Him exactly how you feel.

> *God is the author of all human emotions. If anyone understands your anger, it's God!*

FOR REFLECTION OR DISCUSSION

Do you agree that "anger is neither right or wrong; it's just a feeling"?

My journal . . .

The Cancer Chapter

*Wherever your treasure is, there the desires of
your heart will also be.*

LUKE 12:34

Etymology, the study of the origin of words, tells us
that the English words *author* and *authority* both
come from the same Latin word, *auctor.* It also tells us
that in times past, the word *authority* meant "author
whose statements are regarded as correct."[1]

To Christians, Jesus is both Authority and Author. He
is the supreme authority in the universe, and the "author
whose statements are regarded as correct," because it was
He who inspired the infallible words of the Bible. He is
the author of all creation, including every human life. In
the book of Hebrews, He is called the "author of eternal
salvation,"[2] and the "author and finisher of our faith."[3]

To frame those truths in more personal terms, Jesus
is the author of your story and the days of your life are
the pages of His manuscript. Since the moment you
were conceived, He has been writing every chapter of

your story, including the one you are living right now: the cancer chapter. You never saw this chapter coming, of course, but it's a very important part of your story. What happens in this chapter can inspire the remaining chapters of your book. This is because cancer often forever changes how people look at life. For many, and perhaps for you, cancer is an attention-getting, priority-rearranging wakeup call. Pursuits and pleasures that once seemed vitally important may have quickly paled in the light of your cancer diagnosis. God may now have your full attention in a way He has never had it before, causing you to rethink some things and question others.

For many Christ followers, the cancer experience transforms an anemic walk with God into something like oxygen, something they pant for and long for with a fervency that they lacked before. And as their "cancer chapter" deepens their love for God, many begin to also think differently about what *treasure* really is (Luke 12:34, above).

Before Dwight was diagnosed with cancer, he had already begun reevaluating his priorities. Although he had been a Christ follower since childhood, much of his adult life had centered around career achievements and the material rewards of success: "the right education, the right house, the right car." He admits, "I just got caught up in the ways of the world." With the diagnosis of cancer, his priorities quickly came into sharper focus.

"A number of goals don't seem as important now," he said. "I don't have that CEO desire anymore. It's a completely different mindset. My plan now is not to focus on me. My plan is to focus on whatever God wants me to do." He has concluded that "It's really about relationships. Because in the end, your relationship with God and your relationships with your fellow man are the treasures."

The person who starts the race is not the same person who finishes the race.
—ANONYMOUS

FOR REFLECTION OR DISCUSSION

Is your cancer chapter changing what you treasure?

My journal . . .

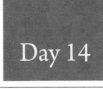

Day 14

Sar-Shalom

And he will be called: Wonderful Counselor, Mighty God,
Everlasting Father, Prince of Peace.

ISAIAH 9:6

In Old Testament times, names were highly significant. In the Hebrew culture, names were often intended to describe one's true essence. It's not surprising, then, that the name of the promised Messiah revealed in Isaiah 9:6 is an astonishing revelation of the true essence of God the Son. In this verse, the words, Wonderful Counselor, Mighty God, Everlasting Father, Prince of Peace, do not merely *describe* Jesus, they are, in fact, actually His *name.* That is, His full name is *wonderful counselor-mighty God-everlasting Father-prince of peace.* In Hebrew, the name is *Pele-yoez-El-gibbor-Abi-ad-Sar-Shalom.* This name declares the true essence of our Savior.

Each of the four segments of this compound name is like a facet of a diamond, revealing a different aspect of the beautiful, flawless character and divine nature of God:[1]

- *Pele-yoez* (**wonderful-counselor**) is the extraordinary One who not only counsels but powerfully executes wondrous and miraculous things. He is the One whose teaching astonished those who heard Him (Matthew 7:28).

- *El-gibbor* (**God-the-Mighty-One**) is our mighty Hero-God, the powerful warrior of the universe who possesses superhuman wisdom and strength. He is God Almighty wrapped in human flesh. Nothing is too hard for *El-gibbor* (Jeremiah 32:17).

- *Abi-ad* (**Father of Eternity**), now and forever, acts as a Father toward us, His children. This Father protects and provides for all who are His. This Father's promises are irrevocable, worthy of our trust even when earthly circumstances ensnarl us in doubt. His kingdom, our eternal home, has no end (Luke 1:33).

The final compound name, *Sar-Shalom,* appears in only this one verse of the Bible. Sar usually means subordinate official. But since this is God, it means He is *the* official, the One in charge. He is Sar-Shalom, the One in charge of shalom. Shalom means peace, but the meaning is far richer than most people realize. In the truest sense of the word, shalom means *complete peace*: wholeness, contentment, security, harmony, and prosperity. It is characterized by tranquility, safety, and an orderly personal life. It means freedom from agitation and discord. To experience true shalom is to be at peace within oneself, at peace with others, and at peace with God.

Sar-Shalom has special significance for everyone living with cancer. The cancer journey forces people to grapple with many difficult emotions and most will experience their share of anxious moments. Coping with cancer can make people weary and thirsty for peace, longing to return to the sense of well-being they once had. Dr. Skip Moen has described Jesus, this official in charge of shalom, as the "well-being authority." He said, "If you really want shalom, then you must come to him, for he is the one divinely ordained to give it. . . . No effort toward well-being is accomplished without the expressed authority of Jesus."[2]

Jesus not only gives this peace, He *is* this peace! His name is Prince of Peace, Sar-Shalom, the perfect peace of God. He wants you to share in this peace. He said, "I am leaving you with a gift—peace of mind and heart. And the peace I give is a gift the world cannot give."[3]

The more you yield to Sar-Shalom, the more you will experience the same peace that exists in Christ's own inner being: "the fruit of the Spirit is . . . peace."[4] This peace is available to you right now and on each day of your journey through cancer.

*Peace I leave with you; My [perfect] peace I
give to you; not as the world gives do I give to you.
Do not let your heart be troubled, nor let
it be afraid. [Let My perfect peace calm you in
every circumstance and give you courage
and strength for every challenge.]*
—JESUS, JOHN 14:27 AMP

FOR REFLECTION OR DISCUSSION

Is there anything keeping you from resting in the perfect
peace of Sar-Shalom?

My journal . . .

Grateful

I will exalt You, my God, O King,
And [with gratitude and submissive wonder]
I will bless Your name forever and ever.

PSALM 145:1 AMP

At some point in their cancer journey, many people discover within themselves a rather surprising by-product of their illness: gratitude. Gratitude, according to the Merriam-Webster dictionary, is "the state of being grateful," and *grateful* is defined as "appreciative of benefits received."

Grateful is the very word that Lee used to describe how he feels looking back on both his and his wife's very difficult experiences with cancer. He said, "Grateful, gosh, so grateful. Every day that I wake up it's, 'God, thanks so much. I get another day.' Through all these medical events, our faith changed over time. It became stronger for both of us. We became more intentional about our faith, church, and all of its activities. Our Christian friends became more important to us. I think our life became a lot better." If they had never experienced cancer, he said, "I'm sure we would have continued to go to church, but there's a difference between 'I'm a regular churchgoer' and 'I'm on fire for Jesus.' Gratitude helped lift my recurring depression about it all."

Facing cancer has also made Jonathan profoundly grateful. "Cancer made me start living now how I wish I would have always lived," he said. "Cancer hasn't changed how I view God, but it has certainly changed me. It has made me thankful for things that I just always took for granted. Like, I could not imagine a man having a better wife than I have. She is the best wife that any man could ever ask for, the best mom any kid could ever ask for. And my boys, I love them more than life itself. Why did it take cancer to make me realize how blessed I was? I hate that it took cancer to open my eyes, to stop looking at what I didn't have and realize what I do have."

Laura and Keela both still have their "attitude of gratitude" intact, despite the fact that each was already dealing with another major life event when her cancer was diagnosed. Even though it was difficult for Laura to care for her newborn baby during her cancer treatments, she focused on the things for which she was grateful. She reflected, "Yes, I have cancer, but I'm able to be with my son every single day and watch him grow and learn. Yes, I have no hair, but I have to be thankful that I am able to drive myself to the hospital and walk in there by myself."

Keela's second bout with breast cancer could not have come at a worse time. Her family was still trying to regain its balance in the wake of an unexpected adversity. Then, right after Keela's diagnosis, another family member also experienced a serious health crisis.

Despite this series of extremely difficult circumstances, Keela, her husband, and her children have forged a deeper bond for which she is profoundly grateful. She said, "My husband and I are just so thankful for every day. I think it's definitely made that relationship a lot stronger and it's really brought us closer together. We have always been a pretty close family, but it's made us realize how important that family support is."

Has having cancer sparked gratitude within you? If so, or *especially* if not, here is a challenge, an assignment, if you will: imagine your heart as a garden space where you can plant seeds of gratitude. What can you be grateful for? Who can you be grateful for? What is happening right now that you can be grateful for? Whether you are in a hospital room, in your own living room, or on a beach gazing out over the ocean, see, hear, taste, touch, and smell the world around you. Find three things for which you can be grateful in this moment. Then plant those seeds of gratitude deep in the garden of your heart. You can record what you planted in the journaling space below if you like.

Here's the thing to keep in mind: seeds produce fruit, and fruit contains more seeds. So ponder the implications of this verse: " . . . a farmer who plants only a few seeds will get a small crop. But the one who plants generously will get a generous crop" (2 Corinthians 9:6).

Why did it take cancer to make me realize how blessed I was?
—JONATHAN

FOR REFLECTION OR DISCUSSION

What might happen if you planted seeds of gratitude in your heart every day?

My journal . . .

Day 16

Sing!

But as for me, I will sing about your power. Each morning I will sing with joy about your unfailing love. For you have been my refuge, a place of safety when I am in distress.

PSALM 59:16

God loves it when we sing praises to Him. Many verses in both the Old and New Testament speak of singing to the Lord:

Psalm 47:6
Sing praises to God, sing praises; sing praises to our King, sing praises!

Isaiah 12:5
Sing to the LORD, for he has done wonderful things. Make known his praise around the world.

Ephesians 5:18–19
Be filled with the Holy Spirit, singing psalms and hymns and spiritual songs among yourselves, and making music to the Lord in your hearts.

Colossians 3:16
Let the message about Christ, in all its richness, fill your lives. . . . Sing psalms and hymns and spiritual songs to God with thankful hearts.

In his article "Seven Biblical Reasons Why Singing Matters,"[1] Tom Olson points out that singing is a way to infuse your life with the richness of God's Word, as instructed in Colossians 3:16 above. Whether you prefer traditional hymns, contemporary Christian music, or an eclectic blend of both, singing "spiritual songs to God" helps you internalize biblical truths.

Olson also says that God wants us to sing "psalms and hymns and spiritual songs" because this helps us align ourselves with the will of God. He observed, "It's very hard to lie, be greedy or to look at something inappropriate" when you are making music to the Lord in your heart. A heart that is praising God in song, he notes, "will not easily give in to temptation."

When you feel well and happy, it's easy and natural to sing out your praises to God. However, a bad night's sleep, pain, fatigue, or the effects of chemo can put a damper on your desire to sing to the Lord. Sometimes when you don't feel like singing praise, speaking praise, or even silently praising God, it's good to go ahead and do it anyway, according to Hebrews 13:15. This verse says, "Therefore, let us offer through Jesus a continual *sacrifice of praise* to God, proclaiming our allegiance to his name" (italics added). A "sacrifice of praise" is praise that costs you something. When you speak or sing praise to God even though you are weary or feeling unwell, you are offering a sacrifice of praise because you have willingly stepped beyond your comfort zone to do it.

Sacrificially singing praise to God has a way of instilling courage as the singer hears his or her words affirm that "God's got this!" Chapter 20 of 2 Chronicles records a great example of this. The nation of Judah was being invaded. As King Jehoshaphat was sending his army into battle, he provided powerful encouragement for his troops when he "appointed men to sing to the LORD and to praise him for the splendor of his holiness as they went out at the head of the army, saying: 'Give thanks to the LORD, for his love endures forever'" (v. 21 NIV).

The result? You guessed it—victory! "As they began to sing and praise, the LORD set ambushes against the men of Ammon and Moab and Mount Seir who were invading Judah, and they were defeated."[2]

On your most difficult days, you may find that you are simply too weary to sing. On those days, turn to the book of Psalms. In ancient times, the psalms were set to music. Now, those same psalms can be your "silent hymnbook," allowing you to worship God without music or voice. As your heart sings its silent praise in the context of your cancer, you may find yourself saying of the psalms, as pastor Steven J. Cole did, "There is no other book in the Bible where I have personally found more help in the crises of life."[3]

Therefore, let us offer through Jesus a continual sacrifice of praise to God, proclaiming our allegiance to his name.
—HEBREWS 13:15

FOR REFLECTION OR DISCUSSION

What sacrifice of praise can you sing, speak, or silently offer to the Lord today?

My journal . . .

Day 17

Brain Fog

You know when I sit down and when I rise up
[my entire life, everything I do];
You understand my thought from afar.
PSALM 139:2 AMP

One of the most irksome and challenging side effects of many cancer treatments is "brain fog." Brain fog is the hazy thinking, lack of focus, and memory problems that sometimes result from treatments such as radiation or hormone therapy. Those who experience it after chemotherapy often refer to it as "chemo brain." No matter what you call it, as Melody pointed out, "It's very, very real. I still have it and it's frustrating." Dwight also described it as "frustrating," especially, he said, "when you're used to being sharp, quick, and able to think of words that you want to use. When people don't know you, and you're sort of struggling, they don't realize what the cause is. And so you have a choice: either try to explain or just let it go." Jeff agrees. "I struggle with remembering stuff. It's embarrassing," he said.

Brain fog makes everyday life more difficult for many with cancer. Dwight said, "It just adds to all the other challenges you are facing." Forgotten appointments, misplaced keys, difficulties with multitasking, and slowed thinking can all be due to brain fog. Unfortunately, rest does not help. While resting does help the body fight cancer, it doesn't improve brain fog or take away the fatigue that often accompanies it.

While cancer treatments don't cause brain fog for everyone, it is a relatively common problem. When *ProstateCancer.net* asked online readers, "Is brain fog a side effect of hormone therapy or chemo?" one hundred and thirty people took time to comment.[1] When this same website invited visitors to answer the question, "Have you experienced any memory problems since starting your treatment?" more than 670 men participated in the poll. Their responses (as of December 2019)[2] were:

437 (65%): yes
152 (23%): no
81 (12%): I am not sure

If you are dealing with cognitive side effects from your treatments, it is immensely comforting to remember that God sees right through your brain fog or "chemo brain." He completely understands your thoughts even when you aren't sure about them yourself. He not only understands your thinking, but the intents of your heart as well. In all the universe, the only one who knows your mind this perfectly is your omniscient (all-knowing) creator. David's words in Psalm 139:1–4 describe God's perfect knowledge of you and His constant presence with you:

> O LORD, you have examined my heart
>   and know everything about me.
> You know when I sit down or stand up.
>   You know my thoughts even when I'm far away.
> You see me when I travel and when I rest at home.
>   You know everything I do.
> You know what I am going to say
>   even before I say it, LORD.

This beautiful psalm is your assurance that when you cannot find the right word, God knows what you mean. When you can't remember, God does, and in perfect detail. When you can't find your phone, He knows exactly where it is (and you can ask Him to help you find it). When you can't concentrate or can't get organized, the God who ordered the universe has an infinite supply of patience to guide you in completing everything you need to do.

In this "foggy" season of your life, you have an opportunity to trust God differently than you have ever needed to trust Him before. Let God's wisdom, poured from the first-century pen of the apostle Paul, encourage you whenever brain fog clouds your way:

I pray that from his glorious, unlimited resources he will empower you with inner strength through his Spirit.

(EPHESIANS 3:16)

Trust in the LORD with all your heart; do not depend on your own understanding. Seek his will in all you do, and he will show you which path to take.

(PROVERBS 3:5-6)

The Holy Spirit helps us in our weakness.

(ROMANS 8:26)

In this "foggy" season of your life, you have an opportunity to trust God differently than you have ever needed to trust Him before.

Has your experience with brain fog increased your empathy for those with other kinds of cognitive issues?

My journal . . .

Day 18

Jehovah-Rapha

*Bless the L*ORD, *O my soul, and forget not all his benefits,*
who forgives all your iniquity, who heals all your diseases.
PSALM 103:2–3 ESV

All tangible things are subject to the laws that God established to govern the physical world He created. If we toss something up in the air, it returns to the ground because of the law of gravity. Plants turn toward the sun because they need its light to grow. All the laws of physics prevail as well. As physical creatures living in this physical world, human beings are also subject to the physical laws that God established. Our bodies are predictably impacted by the realities of our physical environment. If we stay too long in the sun, our skin gets burned. If we climb high up on a mountain where the air is thin, our breathing becomes labored due to the lack of oxygen. If we cut a finger while slicing an onion, blood seeps out as we breach the barrier of our skin. For as long as we live in this physical world, we are subject to the physical laws that govern it.

Because God created all of these physical laws, He can suspend them any time He wants to, and use them in any way He wishes. When God suspends a law He created, we call it "a miracle." For example, consider God's miraculous answer to Joshua's prayer:

> On the day the LORD gave the Israelites victory over the Amorites, Joshua prayed to the LORD in front of all the people of Israel. He said, "Let the sun stand still over Gibeon, and the moon over the valley of Aijalon." So the sun stood still and the moon stayed in place until the nation of Israel had defeated its enemies.
> ... The sun stayed in the middle of the sky, and it did not set as on a normal day. There has never been a day like this one before or since, when the LORD answered such a prayer. (Joshua 10:12–14)

God can also miraculously suspend the natural laws that govern the human body. The most spectacular example of this is, of course, the resurrection of Christ. Jesus died and came back to life, demonstrating God's absolute sovereignty even over death. In the Old Testament, a very striking miracle of healing is found in 2 Kings 20:1–7. King Hezekiah was very sick and God sent the prophet Isaiah to him with bad news: "You will not recover from this illness." Hezekiah wept and poured out his heart to God in prayer. Before Isaiah had even left the King's courtyard, God gave him another message: "Go back to Hezekiah, the leader of my people. Tell him, '. . . I have heard your prayer and seen your tears. I will heal you, and three days from now you will get out of bed and go to the Temple of the LORD. I will add fifteen years to your life.'"

God's response to Hezekiah reveals a compassionate aspect of His divine character: He is Jehovah-Rapha, a name that means *the Lord who heals you.*

But notice *how* Jehovah-Rapha healed Hezekiah. He did not "zap" him with an instant cure. Rather, Hezekiah was healed, apparently over a period of three days, as he received what God led Isaiah to prescribe: "an ointment from figs." The Bible reports, "Hezekiah's servants spread the ointment over the boil, and Hezekiah recovered!" A similar thing occurred in John 9:6. Jesus spit on the ground, made mud with His saliva, and put the mud on the eyes of a blind man. He told the man to go wash in the Pool of Siloam. The next verse says, "So the man went and washed and came back seeing!" From these examples, we see that sometimes Jehovah-Rapha allows us to participate in the "ordinary miracle" of our own healing, which He accomplishes through the doctors and treatments He places in our path.

Psalm 103 promises that Jehovah-Rapha "heals all your diseases." Yet we all know people who prayed for healing but did not receive it. This is troubling—until we consider it from an eternal perspective. Robert Murray M'Cheyne helps us here. He said, "God will either give you what you ask, or something far better."[1] When Jehovah-Rapha, whose very name is *the Lord who heals you,* chooses *not* to heal a Christ follower, He has in mind healing that is infinitely better than we have asked for—our *ultimate* healing in the presence of God. Understanding this has settled the matter for Jeff. He said, "God's Word is going to come true one way or the other. I'm either healed on this side of heaven or the other."

> *God will either give you what you ask*
> *or something far better.*
> —ROBERT MURRAY M'CHEYNE (1813–1843)

FOR REFLECTION OR DISCUSSION

Do you agree with Robert Murray M'Cheyne? With Jeff?

My journal . . .

Day 19

New Clothes

And all who have been united with Christ in baptism have put on Christ, like putting on new clothes.

GALATIANS 3:27

There is nothing from which God cannot bring glory to Himself. That includes cancer, especially when the cancer is being gracefully born by a believer "clothed" in Christ. When cancer patients "put on Christ, like putting on new clothes," they embody an authentic, faith-driven approach to cancer that can impact others, even when they have no idea that others are watching.

This was the kind of impact that Ric had on Dwight. Ric and his wife, Anne, had invited some friends to their home for dinner. After the meal, Ric shared openly about his prostate cancer diagnosis. Dwight recalled, "I saw how he leaned on the Lord, and that he walked with Him, and that he fully trusted in the Lord. And that gave me a great example to follow." Little did anyone know how important Ric's "great example" would soon become to Dwight. Only weeks later, Dwight was also diagnosed with prostate cancer.

"As we get closer to the Lord, He prepares us to be able to handle the next challenge," Dwight said. "I'd gone through difficult trials regarding employment, and the Lord had really worked on major areas in my life. So I believe that He had already put the foundation in me to be able to recognize that He knows what's best and to accept whatever that is." Even so, Dwight said, "I don't know how I would have handled prostate cancer before I saw my friend Ric experience it. Even though his cancer was not as aggressive as mine, and whether it was intentional or not on his part, Ric set the stage for me in how he responded."

Ric, of course, had no idea that the way he was facing his cancer would soon help prepare Dwight to do the same. But that's exactly what happened. By simply approaching his cancer with sincere trust in God, Ric created what pastor and author Michael J. Easley calls "imperceptible influence." Easley, who suffers with chronic back pain due to degenerative disc disease, has written:

> You and I have no idea how we are being used by Christ. Simply pressing on, staying in the Word, choosing not to whine, learning to have a healthy sense of humor in the midst of trials, affirming others in their gifting, and trying to encourage those

*who struggle in similar situations are ways Christ
works through us. Your faithfulness to him and your
compassion for others may never be graded in this
life, but don't underestimate the possibility that God
is using you and that you have that imperceptible
influence. It seems to me that this is much like faith:
"the evidence of things we cannot see"*
(Hebrews 11:1).[1]

To be clothed in Christ means that we have ex-
changed the worn, soiled "old clothes" of life apart from
Christ for the "new clothes" that give evidence of the
Holy Spirit's presence within us. Martin Luther's Bible
Commentary tells us, "With this change of garments a
new birth, a new life stirs in us. New affections toward
God spring up in the heart. New determinations affect
our will."[2] These are the "new clothes" that enable you
to have an imperceptible influence as you simply walk
close to the Lord throughout your cancer journey.

*Don't underestimate the possibility that God is using you
and that you have that imperceptible influence.*
—MICHAEL J. EASLEY

FOR REFLECTION OR DISCUSSION

Whose imperceptible influence has impacted your life?

My journal . . .

Prayer

O You who hear prayer, to You all mankind comes.
PSALM 65:2 AMP

Prayer is perhaps most simply defined as just talking to God. "Talking to God" was Keela's strategy for getting through DIBH—deep inspiration breath-hold—during her daily breast cancer radiation treatments. With the DIBH technique, the patient takes a deep breath and holds that breath until the radiation is delivered. In Keela's case, each breath-hold lasted up to thirty or forty seconds. The deep breath-hold expands the lungs, moving the heart away from the chest. The goal is to get the heart out of the radiation's path in order to minimize the amount of potentially damaging radiation that reaches it and other healthy tissue.[1] During each of her thirty radiation treatments, Keela did fourteen deep breath-holds. Each time she held her breath, she prayed for a different person. Over her six-week course of radiation treatments, Keela's breath-hold "talks with God" added up to 420 separate prayers!

Breath-hold praying was a creative expression of Keela's high regard for intercessory prayer. She said, "I so believe in the power of prayer. I think that the more praying people you have in your corner, the better off you are. My walk with God is just a personal relationship with Him and my prayer time with Him."

When Keela finally rang the bell to celebrate the end of her cancer journey, she officially joined millions of other cancer survivors, some of whom, like her, have been down this road more than once. How did she get through it all? "Pray and pray and pray, and of course, lean on your family too," she said.

The Bible has much to say about prayer. It is amazing to realize that the God of the universe invites us to come to Him in prayer so that He may compassionately listen as we pour out our needs and hurts and requests to Him:

> *So let us come boldly to the throne of our gracious God. There we will receive his mercy, and we will find grace to help us when we need it most. (Hebrews 4:16)*

> *You parents—if your children ask for a loaf of bread, do you give them a stone instead? Or if they ask for a fish, do you give them a snake? Of course not! So if you sinful people know how to give good gifts to your children, how much more will your heavenly Father give good gifts to those who ask him. (Matthew 7:9–11)*

Don't worry about anything; instead, pray about everything. Tell God what you need, and thank him for all he has done. (Philippians 4:6)

Even more amazing is the fact that God the Holy Spirit prays *for you*:

And the Holy Spirit helps us in our weakness. For example, we don't know what God wants us to pray for. But the Holy Spirit prays for us with groanings that cannot be expressed in words. And the Father who knows all hearts knows what the Spirit is saying, for the Spirit pleads for us believers in harmony with God's own will. (Romans 8:26–27)

There is so much comfort in this verse! When you don't know what decision to make, when you are too weak or fatigued or overwhelmed to pray, when you just can't put your feelings into words, remember that the Holy Spirit prays for you. He knows every concern on your heart and every detail of God's perfect will for your life. He faithfully carries even your unspoken prayers to the Father and intercedes lovingly, compassionately, and perfectly on your behalf.

Prayer does not fit us for the greater work;
prayer is the greater work.
—OSWALD CHAMBERS (1874–1917)

FOR REFLECTION OR DISCUSSION

What role would you like prayer to play in your journey
through cancer?

My journal . . .

Look Up

I look up to the mountains—does my help come from there?
My help comes from the LORD, who made heaven and earth!
PSALM 121:1–2

What could be more important than the prayer you have held before God day and night? That thing that robs you of sleep. Burdens your heart. Frightens you. Maybe it's your cancer, 100 percent. Or maybe it's cancer *plus* something else. Overwhelming debt that has you on the verge of bankruptcy. A stressed-to-the-max marriage. The need for mercy from the court. Or maybe it's something so personal and perplexing that you don't even know where to turn. What could possibly be more important than fixing or healing any or all of that?

There is only one thing that matters more, and it's not about your health or your money or your circumstances. It's about you. What matters more is who you will be when your circumstances finally change. When they do, what kind of person will you be? Will your adversities have made you bitter, or will you be better? Will your heart be harder or softer toward others? Will you be more in love with Jesus or will your faith have grown cold? What matters even more than how your situation turns out is how *you* turn out.

And what determines that? Likely, it will be where your heart ultimately seeks its rest.

Sometimes hearts get stalled for a while, longing for a do-over and rehearsing regrets: *If only I had done this instead of that, things would be different . . .*

If only I had walked away while I had the chance . . .

If only I had said no . . .

If only I had said yes . . .

If only I had taken better care of myself . . .

If only I had seen the signs . . .

Sometimes hearts sit for a while, forlorn and dejected, in front of closed doors that hold no hope for a do-over:

The mastectomy has been done.

Everything was lost in the fire.

The leg cannot be saved.

The other candidate got the job.

The divorce is final.

In an interview about her song "Look Up, Child," Lauren Daigle said, "In the moments when we don't have it nailed, when we don't have it figured out, what is the one thing that we could do? *Look up.*"[1] She is right. No matter how overwhelmed with disappointment or heartbreak or regret you may be, you can look up and turn (or return) your life to God. When you do, a surprising do-over of a heavenly sort awaits you.

It's the do-over the great preacher D. L. Moody had in mind when he said, "Let God have your life; He can do more with it than you can."[2] This is the ultimate do-over, more like a life reboot: handing over to God all that is past, all your present circumstances, and all the unknowns of the future. Throw down an anchor into the shifting sands around you and trust God. *Look up!*

> *Let God have your life; He can do more*
> *with it than you can.*
> —D. L. MOODY (1837–1899)

FOR REFLECTION OR DISCUSSION

What matters even more than how your situation turns out is how *you* turn out.

My journal . . .

Day 22

Overwhelmed

When I am overwhelmed, you alone
know the way I should turn.

PSALM 142:3a

Do you sometimes feel overwhelmed by your cancer diagnosis, your treatments, and everything
that is turning your plans and your life upside down?
If so, you may relate to David the psalmist. During one
of the hardest times in his life, David wrote a heartfelt
prayer to God that began,

> *Listen to my prayer, O God.*
>   *Do not ignore my cry for help!*
> *Please listen and answer me,*
>   *for I am overwhelmed by my troubles. . . .*
>
> *Fear and trembling overwhelm me,*
>   *and I can't stop shaking.* (Psalm 55:1–2, 5)

It's not uncommon to feel overwhelmed by cancer, especially at first, when you're trying to wrap your head around it all. Sheryl's advice to every newly diagnosed person is "Just step back and give yourself some time. Don't be overwhelmed by everything. You're not going to understand it all at once. Gather up information and listen to what people are saying, but don't try to process it all at once. Write stuff down because you're not going to be able to remember it all at first. Later on, you will. You're going to understand all the terms, all the medications, the whole process, all the new stuff you're being hit with."

If you feel as overwhelmed by cancer as David was by his troubles, perhaps what he wrote next expresses how you feel too:

> *Oh, that I had wings like a dove;*
> *then I would fly away and rest!*
> *I would fly far away*
> *to the quiet of the wilderness.* (Psalm 55:6–7)

When life feels overwhelming, it's normal to wish to escape our problems, just as David longed to do. However, there is no easy detour around cancer. Most of the time, the only highway that leads to the destination called "cancer free" is the one that involves treatments—and time.

As you travel along on your cancer journey, it's likely that someone, seeking to encourage you, will tell you, "God won't give you more than you can handle." While that certainly sounds like truth, it isn't. As Jeff correctly noted, "I see nothing scriptural to support that." What the Bible *actually* says is not about escaping difficulties, but about escaping temptation: "And God is faithful. He will not allow the temptation to be more than you can stand. When you are tempted, he will show you a way out so that you can endure" (1 Corinthians 10:13). As Christians, we serve a God of truth. In fact, Jesus Himself said He *is* truth: "I am the way, the truth, and the life . . . " (John 14:6). So truth matters, and the truth is that God *does* sometimes give us more than we in our humanness can handle. He does it out of His great love for us, so that we will discover our powerlessness and turn to our God in humility, realizing that only He can carry our burden and give us the wisdom to lean on His strength, not our own, to make it through our trials, whatever they may be. Jeff said, "God wants us to be dependent on Him. This is our freedom in Jesus Christ. That's how I have been led to believe in my times with God."

So often, we just want God to change our circumstances. But God is always far more interested in using our circumstances to change *us*. That inner transformation occurs as we place our whole lives in His faithful, loving, more-than-capable hands. As the great nineteenth-century preacher Charles Spurgeon wrote, "Oh, think not, believer, that your sorrows are out of God's plan; they are necessary parts of it."[1]

> *Give all your worries and cares to God,*
> *for he cares about you.*
> —1 PETER 5:7

FOR REFLECTION OR DISCUSSION

So often, we just want God to change our circumstances. But God is always far more interested in using our circumstances to change *us*.

My journal . . .

Day 23

Gorgeous

*"The LORD doesn't see things the way you see them.
People judge by outward appearance, but the
LORD looks at the heart."*

1 SAMUEL 16:7

Cancer or its treatments changed the appearance of
some of the people who were interviewed for this
book. Laura's chemotherapy caused her beautiful blonde
hair to fall out. Jeff's striking change in appearance is due
to weight loss. Dwight will have permanent reminders of
his cancer in the tattoos that were used to mark his body
for radiation. For Melody and Keela, their mastectomies
will be lifelong reminders of cancer. For others, cancer
creates scars, rashes, postural changes, or changes in nails
or skin tone. Many also deal with the physical effects of
cancer that are not so visible, such as debilitating fatigue,
difficulty sleeping, changes in appetite, numbness, pain,
incontinence, impotence, or infertility.

Any one of these physical changes, or a combination
of them, can significantly impact a person's *body image*.

Body image is defined on the Livestrong website as simply "what you believe about your appearance."[1] Body image is "psychosocial," meaning that it affects a person both psychologically and in the way they interact with friends, family, and others they encounter socially. Whether the changes caused by cancer are temporary or permanent, and whether they are visible to others or not, they can make a person feel ashamed of his or her body, self-conscious, anxious, or insecure. These changes can also cause grief or create a sense of being different from other people. One analysis of data from the American Cancer Society found that body image dissatisfaction following cancer treatment is common among both men and women.[2]

Livestrong encourages those struggling with their body image to remember that "your body is only one part of who you are as a whole person. If you focus only on what your body looks like, you might overlook the strength of your personality, your interest in life and the talents you bring to many areas of your life."[3] Those are wise words, and for Christians, there's something else, something even more important, to keep in mind. It's the truth of 1 Samuel 16:7, the theme verse above: God values inner beauty far more than He values outer beauty. He is not looking at your outer appearance; He is looking at your heart. As Matthew Henry observed in his commentary on this verse, "We can tell how men look, but he can tell what they are."[4] In the New Testament, Peter underscored this idea when he wrote to women, "Don't be concerned about the outward beauty of fancy hairstyles, expensive jewelry, or beautiful clothes. You should clothe yourselves instead with the beauty that comes from within, the unfading beauty of a gentle and quiet spirit, which is so precious to God" (1 Peter 3:3–4).

Whenever you must bear up under any painful, frightening, or dreaded physical or emotional impact from cancer, draw very near to the Lord, mindful that His gaze rests continually upon your heart. He is watching the amazing transformation that is slowly taking place within you. Tim Keller described that precious transformation when he wrote, "A lump of coal under pressure becomes a diamond. And the suffering of a person in Christ only turns you into somebody gorgeous."[5]

God values inner beauty far more than He values outer beauty.

FOR REFLECTION OR DISCUSSION

How does your body image impact you emotionally, socially, and spiritually?

My journal . . .

Day 24

Jonathan and Jehoshaphat

". . . the battle is not yours, but God's."
2 CHRONICLES 20:15

Yo u have a tumor in your left eye. You have what's called ocular melanoma. In other words," the doctor said, "you have cancer."

Jonathan said, "You don't ever want to have a doctor look at you and utter those three dreaded words. And you especially don't want to hear them when you're forty-five and have two boys in high school. But that's where I was." Nevertheless, when his doctor spoke those three dreaded words, Jonathan recalled, "I felt strikingly calm. As a Christian, I just know God is in control."

Ocular melanoma is a rare cancer. In the United States, only about 2,500 people are diagnosed with it each year. In about half of all cases, ocular melanoma spreads to other parts of the body, most often to the liver. Once it spreads, it is usually fatal. In some people it spreads quickly; in others, it may not spread for ten to fifteen years or longer.[1]

So far, Jonathan's cancer has responded very well to treatment and has not spread. This may be partly due to the fact that, early on, he decided to take a proactive approach and do everything in his power to stay healthy. He lost seventy pounds, changed his diet and exercise habits, and incorporated some alternative therapies as well. However, he is quick to point out, "Ultimately, God is in charge." He said, "It's just a constant trusting in God, knowing He is in control of my life."

Even so, Jonathan admits that his uncertain prognosis hangs over him like a cloud, "a burden I will never be free from." He has been greatly encouraged, however, by one particular story in 2 Chronicles, chapter 20. He recounted the story, pointing out with some amazement, "What I'm going through is almost perfectly in line with it."

He said, "Jehoshaphat was king over Judah and Jerusalem. Just doing what kings do, living his life. And that's what I was: I was king; I was enjoying my life, living my life. And then all of a sudden, one day, some people came to Jehoshaphat and said, 'A vast army is coming against you. And they're right over there on the other side of the sea.' And one day, doctors told me, 'A vast army is coming against you. It's not here now. But there's a 72 to 80 percent chance that within five years, it's coming. A vast army is coming against you and it is already formed. It's coming against you.'

"Jehoshaphat did exactly what I did. He inquired of the Lord. And you do that when you find yourself in that situation, when the doctors tell you that there's nothing to do.

"Verse 12 really spoke to me. It says, 'We have no power to face this vast army that is attacking us. We do not know what to do, but our eyes are on you.' So here's Jehoshaphat saying, 'God, I don't know what to do. I don't know what to do! But our eyes are on You.' And I have prayed to God so many times and said, 'God, what do I do?'

"Skipping down to verse 15: 'Do not be afraid or discouraged because of this vast army. For the battle is not yours, but God's. . . . Go out to face them tomorrow, and the LORD will be with you' [vv. 15–16 NIV]. And that army was defeated!

"So it's like the whole story of me. Because I'm just rocking on with life. And then all of a sudden one day I hear, 'Down the road, it's coming.' I turned towards God in shame. In shame, because I shouldn't have had to turn again towards God—I should have already been there. But I wasn't. So I turned towards Him and asked for His forgiveness, His grace, and His mercy, telling Him that I don't know what to do. I know that the battle is not mine, but His.

"Second Chronicles 20—that is my story. It could not

be more perfect. The beginning is the same. The middle is the same. My hope and prayer is that the ending will be the same too."

> *It's just a constant trusting in God, knowing He is in control of my life.*
> —JONATHAN

FOR REFLECTION OR DISCUSSION

How do Jonathan's story and the story in 2 Chronicles compare to your story?

My journal . . .

Day 25

The Hardest Part

*If your gift is serving others, serve them well. If you are a
teacher, teach well. If your gift is to encourage others, be
encouraging. If it is giving, give generously. If God has given
you leadership ability, take the responsibility seriously. And if
you have a gift for showing kindness to others, do it gladly.*

ROMANS 12:7–8

Laura said that throughout her cancer journey,
"People have wanted to do so much. And give so
much. And it's been so hard to accept because you feel
like you're putting them out. That has been the hardest
part—just letting people do something for you."

When Melody had breast cancer the first time, she
was a single mom with four children, two in college and
a six-year-old and an eleven-year-old still at home. "I did
great," she said, "until one day I could barely move. Radiation hits you like a ton of bricks."

After the game-changing "ton of bricks" radiation
treatment, the doctor told Melody, "I'm going to go get
your driver now. I want to talk with them."

"Driver?" Melody asked.

"Don't tell me you've been driving here yourself," said the doctor. "You are not to drive anymore until I tell you that you can drive again."

Melody realized that she was too weak to even start calling people to line up rides. She had to ask friends to do that for her. "That was very humbling," she said.

For many people with cancer, accepting help from others is indeed, as Laura said, the hardest part. Melody shared a story about a woman who called the hospital from her bedroom at home, saying, "I am so sick and I can't stop throwing up." The operator told her they would send an ambulance to come get her. All the while, her husband was at home, sitting right there in the living room. "He had absolutely no idea," Melody said. "That's how much people don't want to ask for help."

"A disease like cancer is so humbling," said Lee, Melody's husband. "It brings you to your knees to the point where you've got to have some help. You've run out of rope. You just can't be proud anymore." The needs that arise due to cancer often force people to humble themselves and let go of pride, which, Lee pointed out, "God wants you to do anyway."

Lee is right, of course. In the book of James, we read, "God sets Himself against the proud and haughty, but gives grace [continually] to the lowly (those who are humble enough to receive it)."[1] But why would this be God's design? Perhaps it is because when a person humbly admits their need, blessing is set in motion—not just for the person needing help, but also for the helper. When pride is replaced with humility, it creates opportunities for others to use their God-given abilities. Those gifted by God for service can now serve. Those with resources to give can now give. Those whom God has gifted to show kindness, give encouragement, or lead can now embrace the opportunities to do so.

When a person with cancer humbly receives the service or gifts of others, blessings sometimes multiply. Laura was "overwhelmed in a good way" when at least 300 people, many whom she did not even know, attended a fundraiser on her behalf. Others brought meals. Coworkers chipped in to help pay for her insurance coverage while she could not work. All of this, said Laura, "is just beyond amazing to me."

Because Laura overcame "the hardest part—just letting people do something for you," others had opportunities to give money, bring meals, help pay for her insurance, and bless her in other ways. As a result of their kindnesses, Laura's greatest desire is now to "pay it forward." She said, "The thing I look forward to the most is to be able to help somebody else."

That's how it's supposed to work!

And all of you, dress yourselves in humility
as you relate to one another, for God opposes the
proud but gives grace to the humble.
—I PETER 5:5

FOR REFLECTION OR DISCUSSION

How are you handling "the hardest part"?

My journal . . .

Rebel Cells

*Joyful are those who obey his laws and search
for him with all their hearts.*

PSALM 119:2

The Bible describes true believers collectively as the "body" of Christ. That is, Christ's followers function as His hands and feet here on earth, carrying out His will. In a letter to the Corinthian church, Paul wrote, "The human body has many parts, but the many parts make up one whole body. So it is with the body of Christ."[1] He explained that God gives different kinds of spiritual gifts to believers because many different functions are needed: "If the whole body were an eye, how would you hear? Or if your whole body were an ear, how would you smell anything? But our bodies have many parts, and God has put each part just where he wants it."[2] Paul wanted believers to understand that just as every part of the human body has a specific, important role, so does each person who is part of the body of Christ.

The human body is most likely to stay healthy when

all of its cells are doing the task they were designed to do. It works the same way in the body of Christ. When each individual believer or "cell" uses his or her spiritual and natural gifts to serve others in love, the Church stays healthy and functions as God intended. That's the goal, but because we have free will, Paul cautions, "do not let your freedom become an opportunity for the sinful nature (worldliness, selfishness), but through love serve and seek the best for one another."[3] When believers reject Paul's warning, choosing instead to indulge their sinful nature, they become "rebel cells" within the body of Christ. As rebels, they are no longer in sync with the purposes of God.

The authors of the book *Foods to Fight Cancer* explain that " . . . cancer is first and foremost a cell disease" and every cancer starts with a "rebel cell." Rebel cells (like rebel Christians) "forget their primary function in the organism as a whole." The authors say that "cancer appears when a cell stops being resigned to playing the role assigned to it and no longer agrees to cooperate with the others to dedicate its resources to the benefit of all the other cells in the organism. This cell becomes an outlaw isolating itself from its fellows and no longer responding to orders from the society in which it lives. Henceforth, it has only one thing on its mind: ensuring its own survival and that of its descendants."[4] So, whether we think of a rebel cell literally, as a physical cell that causes cancer, or metaphorically, as a believer who has "forgotten their function" in the body of Christ, a rebel cell is one that has become selfish. It no longer works for the good of the whole body, but only to fulfill its own self-centered agenda.

The human body consists of more than 37 trillion cells. Among this plethora of cells, all of us have some precancerous cells, each laden with potential to become a rebel cell.[5] Similarly, every Christ follower has the potential to become a rebel cell in the body of Christ. We're all potential rebels because of the lifelong tug-of-war that goes on within us between our new Godly nature, given at salvation, and our old, ungodly nature, inherited from Adam. At every decision point, we determine how the tug-of-war turns out: will we follow the Lord or be a rebel cell?

We glean a powerful spiritual lesson from the cell disease known as cancer. Cancer teaches, in an unforgettable way, that rebel cells bring pain and many problems. If you have cancer, you can understand in a way that others may not, how wise Paul's warning to believers truly is. With apologies to Paul, consider this paraphrase of Galatians 5:13, which incorporates the cell metaphor:

As a beloved cell in Christ's body of believers on earth, do not use your God-given freedom to indulge your selfish, sinful nature. Behaving this way, as a "rebel cell," could harm and greatly sadden your brothers and sisters in Christ. Instead, use your freedom as a healthy cell to sincerely follow God and demonstrate His love by working with the other cells, serving them, and seeking whatever is best for them.

For the entire law is fulfilled in keeping this one command: "Love your neighbor as yourself."
—GALATIANS 5:14 NIV

FOR REFLECTION OR DISCUSSION

What spiritual insights can you gain from your experience with the "rebel cells" of cancer?

My journal . . .

What If?

My future is in your hands.

PSALM 31:15a

What-if questions go hand-in-hand with a cancer diagnosis:

What if I choose the wrong doctor?
What if the treatment doesn't work?
What if I can't handle the side effects?
What if I go through all of this and the cancer
  comes back?

All of these questions grow out of the many uncertainties of living with cancer. You may now feel more insecure than you used to. You may also be frustrated because it's now hard to make plans. If you want to schedule lunch with friends, a what-if emerges: *what if I'm not feeling well that day?* If you want to make airline reservations for your family's vacation, a what-if pops up: *what if my treatment schedule changes?*

When Keela was diagnosed with breast cancer in

2005, she had all of the typical what-if questions. But after successful treatment, including a double mastectomy, all of the what-ifs faded into the background and life returned to normal. For the next twelve years, Keela hardly thought about cancer. Then one day, while massaging her sore chest muscles after a workout, she felt a tiny lump under her arm. In that moment, the most remote of all the what-ifs resurfaced: *What if I go through all of this and the cancer comes back?*

Thinking it was probably not cancer, but wanting to be sure, she scheduled an appointment with her doctor. Tests confirmed that even though Keela's natural breasts were long gone, her breast cancer was indeed back, this time in the lymph nodes under her arm.

Thirty radiation treatments followed. Monday through Friday, for six consecutive weeks, she drove an hour from her home to the treatment center, spent close to an hour there, then after a lunch break, drove an hour back home. "It was hard," she recalls, glad that her radiation is now in the rearview mirror. Her ongoing treatment ("maybe for the rest of my life") is a daily chemotherapy pill.

When "cancer 2.0" was first diagnosed, Keela said, "It was traumatic. I had some bad days and worried a lot." She remembers thinking, "Oh my goodness, is this the one that's going to take me?" But after a few days, her perspective changed. "I just decided it's not my plan; it's

God's plan. And whatever He has, whatever my journey is meant to be, it's going to be. I prayed about it and decided to take the optimistic route and just be thankful that I did catch it early. If it hadn't been for that pulled muscle, it could have been a long time before I caught it."

As Keela's story illustrates, one key to coping with the uncertainties of cancer, including the possibility of its return, is accepting the fact that all of the what-ifs are beyond your control. They are most certainly not beyond the control of God, however, and Keela has placed her life and her future in His care. She said, "I can't imagine going through this and not having a relationship with God, walking this alone." Her advice to fellow travelers on the cancer or "cancer 2.0" journey is, "Lean on God and just know that there's a plan. Be confident in that."

All the days ordained for me were written in your book
before one of them came to be.
—PSALM 139:16b NIV

FOR REFLECTION OR DISCUSSION

Have you placed all of your what-ifs in God's hands?

My journal . . .

Day 28

Fear Not

When I am afraid, I put my trust in you.
PSALM 56:3 ESV

In this fallen world, everyone encounters adversity. Jesus affirmed this when He said, "Here on earth you will have many trials and sorrows. But take heart, because I have overcome the world" (John 16:33). Pastor Charles Stanley has observed that "Fear always accompanies adversity; in fact, a degree of fear is what makes something an adversity instead of just another experience."[1]

Because fear and adversity are so intertwined, it's not surprising that, as Jonathan pointed out, "the Bible says 'Fear not' 365 times . . . once for every day of the year." Some say the number is even higher. Psychologist and "soul care" counselor Bill Gaultiere wrote, "Expanding the search to look at verses encouraging us not to worry or not to be anxious would add many, many more 'Fear not' Scriptures. This is why I say that there are more than 365 'Fear nots' in the Bible."[2]

Most everyone with cancer has felt fearful at one time

or another. Experts say that it's not unusual for people with cancer to not only fear the disease or its treatments, but to also fear being unable to pay their bills, function at their jobs, or take care of their families.

Jonathan admitted, "I know the Bible says 'Fear not.' But I confess that I do fear; I confess that I do worry. I have two boys, one that just graduated high school, and another that's going to be a junior next year. When I think about things like high school and college and weddings and grandkids, the thing that I fear is missing out on all those things." Laura said, "I just worry in general about life now that I've been through this. There is a whole lot higher risk for me developing a second kind of cancer. I think that's just going to stick with me. I'm scared that I may have to go through this again. I may never have any problems. But I know that the chance is higher, so it worries me." She added, "And I know everybody's worried about medical bills. I get it."

One cancer patient said, "We worry about things much more than we need to, because much of what we worry about never comes to fruition." He is right, of course! But it can be difficult to rein in fear and worry. That's why Pastor Rick Warren believes the "fear not" message is repeated so many times throughout the Bible. He thinks it shows that God does not want His children's minds to be clouded by fear.[3]

So when you are feeling fearful, how do you "fear not"?

Perhaps you have heard Joyce Meyer's adage, *Where the mind goes, the man follows.* The idea is that whatever your mind habitually dwells upon—what you meditate on—will guide your choices and decisions. Fear is fed by meditating on scary thoughts; "fear not" is fed by meditating upon God's thoughts, the truths of the Bible. Author Jerry White explained the biblical concept of meditation. "Our minds and imaginations run constantly. They never stop," he said. "Meditation then is a learned skill to focus and concentrate on reading, studying, and reflecting on Scripture. . . . *As I read the Bible, I purposely stop to reflect rather than to rush through.* For example, while studying Romans 12:1–2, I underlined all the verbs and circled the nouns. Then I thought and prayed over each as they applied to my life. *I memorize key Scriptures and review them during the day*, and I pray about a particular verse that speaks to my specific situation at the time."[4]

You can do the very same thing. Choose verses that are comforting and personally significant to you. Ask God to help you glean the full meaning of each verse as you meditate on it. Thoughtfully consider each individual word and phrase as if Jesus were speaking it directly to you. When you're ready, recite the verse over and over, many times a day for as many days as it takes to completely memorize it. Once it is firmly entrenched in your memory, you can call it to mind at any moment, whenever you begin to feel afraid.

If you are not familiar with the Bible, you could start by meditating on and memorizing the three verses included on these "Fear Not" pages. Alternatively, look up verses that contain the word "afraid" or "trust" or "fear" in a concordance (an alphabetical listing of verses at the end of many Bibles). Meditate on and memorize the verses you discover that speak comfort to your heart at this time.

For God has not given us a spirit of fear and timidity, but of power, love, and self-discipline.
—2 TIMOTHY 1:7

FOR REFLECTION OR DISCUSSION

Why does meditating on and memorizing Scripture calm our fears?

My journal . . .

Hope

Be joyful in hope, patient in affliction, faithful in prayer.
ROMANS 12:12 NIV

The Bible tells us that there are three things that will last forever: faith, hope, and love.[1] In contemporary America, we hear a lot about love, especially romantic love. We hear a lot about faith too, especially if we are churchgoers. But we don't hear very much about hope. Since that's the case, a definition is in order. According to the Merriam-Webster dictionary, *hope* is "desire accompanied by expectation of or belief in fulfillment."

Hope plays an important role in living with cancer. The word "hope" was spoken many times by those interviewed for this book:

- "I think that people that are going through this cancer journey are hurting. . . . And I think they are looking for hope."
- "You just hope that once you have finished with the challenges of cancer that you will be back to where you were before."

- "Now there's nothing more I can do except hope it doesn't come back. Hope they got it all."
- "I just felt like giving up, and that there was no hope."
- "As long as you've got God there's hope. We don't give up because the Bible says 'hope, faith, and love' for eternity."

From the Canadian Cancer Society website: "Some people find it easy to be hopeful—it helps them cope with the hard things happening right now. But you might find it hard to find any hope in what is a tough experience. And that's OK. You don't have to pretend to feel a certain way if you don't."[2]

After a person accepts the fact that they have cancer, their thought patterns have a lot to do with sustaining a hopeful outlook as they move forward. Ultimately, there are two possible mindsets from which to approach cancer and all of its many associated problems. Everyone with cancer stands at one or the other of two baselines every time they encounter a new problem on their cancer journey. In the view from one baseline, the problem looms large because it stands in between the person and God. In the view from the other baseline, God looms large because He stands in between the person and the problem. When a person with cancer holds their problem in the foreground of their thinking, they essentially send God to the background. In this scenario, the problem seems dominant, perhaps even eclipsing God from view. In the other scenario, when a person with cancer keeps God in the foreground of their thinking, the problem stays in the background, enabling the person to focus more on God's power and promises. Clearly, this is the mindset that kindles hope!

Hope, once ignited, can segue to new purpose in life. Regarding this, Mark Batterson has written:

> *No one rolls out the red carpet and invites tragedy into their life, but our greatest gifts and passions are often the by-product of our worst tragedies and failures.* Trials have a way of helping us rediscover our purpose in life.[3] (emphasis added)

For anyone wondering what good could come from their having cancer, this is an intriguing and exciting point to ponder. As you pray and read the Bible, ask God to help you keep Him in the foreground of your thinking and to see your cancer through the lens of hope. If Mark Batterson is right, you just might rediscover something about your purpose in life.

*Trials have a way of helping us rediscover
our purpose in life.*
—MARK BATTERSON

FOR REFLECTION OR DISCUSSION

Do your problems stand in between you and God, or
does God stand in between you and your problems?

My journal . . .

What's Next?

... looking forward to what lies ahead ...
PHILIPPIANS 3:13

Sheila wrote a prayer comparing her new cancer-free life to the joy of looking into Jesus' tomb and finding it empty. She said:

> *I feel like Mary Magdalene at your tomb,*
> *But it's me.*
> *I am at the tomb of my cancer-free life,*
> *A phase that has come to its own sudden end.*

If your cancer treatment is successful, one day you too will find yourself staring into the empty tomb of your cancer-free life (hooray!). On that day, your struggle with cancer will end in a victorious personal "Easter" that you can celebrate for the rest of your life.

But whether or not that cancer-free celebration happens for you, you will, like every one of us, one day step across the threshold from this earthly life into what comes next. In that moment of transition, what will matter for eternity won't be your cancer journey; it will be how you responded to the real Easter—the day Jesus walked out of His burial tomb alive. His resurrection proved that He is who He said He was: God incarnate, alive forever, the only one qualified to provide the sacrifice that secures your place in heaven.

Sheila's prayer goes on to say,

> Help me to trust today
> That the best is yet to come.[1]

The Bible tells us that the best *is* yet to come! What lies ahead in eternity is glorious beyond our ability to imagine:

> No eye has seen, no ear has heard,
>   and no mind has imagined
> what God has prepared
>   for those who love him. (1 Corinthians 2:9)

> He will wipe every tear from their eyes. There will be no more death or mourning or crying or pain, for the old order of things has passed away.
>   He who was seated on the throne said, "I am making everything new!" Then he said, "Write this down, for these words are trustworthy and true."
> (Revelation 21:4–5 NIV)

These verses give us a glimpse of heaven! Heaven will be an endless, joy-filled celebration unmarred by crying or pain or sorrow or cancer. Dwight said, "If my life on earth is ended by cancer, then I have a wonderful life to look forward to in heaven. You certainly don't want to leave your loved ones and friends, but you realize that you're going to a better place."

Cancer patients are no strangers to the fears triggered by the pain, problems, and uncertainties of the disease. But no child of God need ever fear what lies beyond the grave. "My fear," Dwight said, "was about the possibility of how fast my cancer could spread. But it was never the fear of dying or fear of what was coming. Unbelievers can't have that perspective. But as a Christian, you have the comfort of the Lord walking with you."

Unlike Dwight, many people with cancer don't allow themselves to think about death. Pastor John Piper, a cancer survivor, warns, "You will waste your cancer if you refuse to think about death." The night before his prostate cancer surgery, Piper wrote a booklet called *Don't Waste Your Cancer*.[2] In it he points out, "Ecclesiastes 7:2 says, 'It is better to go to the house of mourning [a funeral] than to go to the house of feasting, for this is the end of all mankind, and the living will lay it to heart.' How can you lay it to heart if you won't think about it?"

Some people live to be over a hundred; some infants

die before they are born. Every human being has a life span known only to God. It is only the physical body that dies. The human spirit lives on after death; it is eternal. So heed John Piper's advice: don't waste your cancer. Allow yourself to think about the inevitable certainty of death and where you will spend eternity. Dwight said, "There was a point in my life where I thought, 'I'll prepare for that later.' Having cancer has made me realize that 'later' is now."

You may have heard that there are many paths to heaven. The Bible says that, in fact, there is only one: Jesus. He Himself said, "No one can come to the Father except through me" (John 14:6). The Bible affirms this elsewhere: "Salvation is found in no one else, for there is no other name under heaven given to mankind by which we must be saved" (Acts 4:12 NIV).

If you're not sure that heaven will be your eternal home, reach out to Jesus in prayer. In a simple, sincere expression of faith, tell Him you accept that His death on the cross was for you personally and that you believe it paid in full the debt of all your sins. Rest now in the assurance of "what's next"—that one day, with great joy, your Lord will welcome you into heaven.

"No one comes to the Father except through me."
—JESUS

FOR REFLECTION OR DISCUSSION

God wants you to enjoy the comfort and security that come from knowing "what's next!"

My journal . . .

Appendix

30 Selected Scriptures from
Strength for the Cancer Journey

Don't be afraid, for I am with you. Don't be discouraged, for I am your God. I will strengthen you and help you. I will hold you up with my victorious right hand.
—ISAIAH 41:10

The Lord God is my Strength, my personal bravery, and my invincible army; He makes my feet like hinds' feet and will make me to walk [not to stand still in terror, but to walk] and make [spiritual] progress upon my high places [of trouble, suffering, or responsibility]!
—HABAKKUK 3:19 AMPC

He gives power to the weak and strength to the powerless.
—ISAIAH 40:29

I waited patiently for the LORD to help me, and he turned to me and heard my cry.
—PSALM 40:1

For since the world began,
   no ear has heard
and no eye has seen a God like you,
   who works for those who wait for him!
—Isaiah 64:4

The Lord is my shepherd;
   I have all that I need.
He lets me rest in green meadows;
   he leads me beside peaceful streams.
   He renews my strength.
He guides me along right paths,
   bringing honor to his name.
Even when I walk
   through the darkest valley,
I will not be afraid,
   for you are close beside me.
Your rod and your staff
   protect and comfort me.
—Psalm 23:1–4

Jesus Christ is [eternally changeless, always] the same yesterday and today and forever.
—Hebrews 13:8 AMP

God has said, "I will never fail you. I will never abandon you."
—Hebrews 13:5b

Jesus answered, "It is written: 'Man shall not live on bread alone, but on every word that comes from the mouth of God.'"
—MATTHEW 4:4 NIV

For the word of God is alive and powerful. It is sharper than the sharpest two-edged sword, cutting between soul and spirit, between joint and marrow. It exposes our innermost thoughts and desires.
—HEBREWS 4:12

Your word is a lamp to guide my feet and a light for my path.
—PSALM 119:105

Turn to me and be gracious to me, for I am lonely and afflicted.
—PSALM 25:16 NIV

Fix your thoughts on what is true, and honorable, and right, and pure, and lovely, and admirable. Think about things that are excellent and worthy of praise.
—PHILIPPIANS 4:8

You will keep in perfect peace all who trust in you, all whose thoughts are fixed on you!
—ISAIAH 26:3

Peace I leave with you; My [perfect] peace I give to you; not as the world gives do I give to you. Do not let your heart be troubled, nor let it be afraid. [Let My perfect peace calm you in every circumstance and give you courage and strength for every challenge.]
—Jesus, John 14:27 AMP

But as for me, I will sing about your power. Each morning I will sing with joy about your unfailing love. For you have been my refuge, a place of safety when I am in distress.
—Psalm 59:16

Therefore, let us offer through Jesus a continual sacrifice of praise to God, proclaiming our allegiance to his name.
—Hebrews 13:15

You know when I sit down and when I rise up [my entire life, everything I do]; You understand my thought from afar.
—Psalm 139:2 AMP

Trust in the Lord with all your heart; do not depend on your own understanding. Seek his will in all you do, and he will show you which path to take.
—Proverbs 3:5–6

And the Holy Spirit helps us in our weakness. For example, we don't know what God wants us to pray for. But the Holy Spirit prays for us with groanings that cannot be expressed in words. And the Father who knows all hearts knows what the Spirit is saying, for the Spirit pleads for us believers in harmony with God's own will.
—ROMANS 8:26–27

I look up to the mountains—does my help come from there? My help comes from the LORD, who made heaven and earth!
—PSALM 121:1–2

When I am overwhelmed, you alone know the way I should turn.
—PSALM 142:3a

Give all your worries and cares to God, for he cares about you.
—1 PETER 5:7

"Do not be afraid or discouraged because of this vast army. For the battle is not yours, but God's. . . . Go out to face them tomorrow and the Lord will be with you."
—2 CHRONICLES 20:15–17 NIV

My future is in your hands.
—PSALM 31:15a

. . . all the days ordained for me were written in your book before one of them came to be.
—PSALM 139:16b NIV

For God did not give us a spirit of timidity or cowardice or fear, but [He has given us a spirit] of power and of love and of sound judgment and personal discipline [abilities that result in a calm, well-balanced mind and self-control].
—2 TIMOTHY 1:7 AMP

Be joyful in hope, patient in affliction, faithful in prayer.
—ROMANS 12:12 NIV

No one can come to the Father except through me.
—JESUS, JOHN 14:6

So let us come boldly to the throne of our gracious God. There we will receive his mercy, and we will find grace to help us when we need it most.
—HEBREWS 4:16

Additional Verses . . .

Acknowledgments

This book was such a team effort! In addition to my extraordinary "panel of experts," the eight cancer patients to whom the book is dedicated, I want to acknowledge and thank three other groups of people for their contributions. First, I want to thank the cancer survivors and current patients whose kind endorsements appear at the front of the book. I also want to thank those who read early sample devotionals and completed a survey to ensure that the book was on target: Robin Bralley, Ric Wagner, and Jeff, Keela, Dwight, Melody, Lee, and Sheryl from "the panel." Finally, I want to thank my friends who not only carried this project over the finish line with their prayers, but also encouraged me and helped out in other ways. I'm grateful for every one of you: Debbie Gilreath, Dee Johnson, Andrea Buczynski, Ashley McKenzie, Beth Yancey, Beth Lineberry, Carol and Charlie Getty, David Imbrock, Ric and Anne Wagner, Gary Slay, Jan and Jerry Morrison, Dwight Harris, Joe May, Judy and Blair Reins, Marcia Rogers, Steve Sharpe, Terry Chaves, Sam and Vonna Waddell, Melody Salisbury, Linda Hill, and Patricia Julian. I'm also grateful for others, too many to list, who offered words of encouragement and prayer support at various points along the way. A special thank-you goes to Dwight Harris for reading all thirty devotionals and sharing many helpful suggestions.

Above all, always, *Soli Deo gloria!*

Notes

Day 1: Strength for the Journey
1. Chuck Smith, Sermon Notes for 2 Corinthians 12:9, Blue Letter Bible, https://www.blueletterbible.org/Comm/smith_chuck/SermonNotes_2Cr/2Cr_12.cfm?a=1090010.

Day 2: Why, Lord?
1. Matthew 4:23; 8:17.
2. See Joni Eareckson Tada, "A Letter from Joni," in *Beyond Suffering Bible* (Carol Stream, IL: Tyndale, 2016), A8.
3. Lamentations 3:33 AMPC.
4. Jeremiah 29:11.

Day 3: Waiting
1. Attributed to Arnold H. Glasow in "Arnold H Glasow - Some Famous Quotes," Mistral, https://www.mistralassociates.com/glasow_quotes.html.
2. Mrs. Charles E. Cowman, compiler, *Streams in the Desert* (Grand Rapids: Zondervan, 1982), 227.
3. Cortni Marrazzo, "7 Ways God Uses Waiting to Prepare You," https://www.crosswalk.com/faith/spiritual-life/7-ways-god-uses-waiting-to-prepare-you.html.

Day 4: Boundaries
1. Lynn Eib, *50 Days of Hope: Daily Inspiration for Your Journey through Cancer* (Carol Stream, IL: Tyndale, 2012), 9.
2. Proverbs 15:1 ESV.

Day 5: Jehovah-Raah
1. John Gill's Exposition of the Bible, Psalm 23:1, Bible Study Tools, https://www.biblestudytools.com/commentaries/gills-exposition-of-the-bible/psalms-23-1.html.

Day 6: Roots
1. Becky Hughes, "Remembering Billy Graham: His Most Powerful Quotes on Life and Spirituality," https://parade.com/648000/

beckyhughes/remembering-billy-graham-his-most-powerful-
quotes-on-life-and-spirituality/.
2. Robert Murray McCheyne, "Lecture VI," in *The Life and Remains:
Letters, Lectures and Poems of the Rev. Robert Murray Mccheyne,
Minister of St. Peter's Church, Dundee*, 6th ed., ed. Andrew A. Bonar
(New York: Robert Carter, 1848), 402.
3. Dennis Merritt Jones, "Strong Winds Strong Roots: What Trees
Teach Us About Life," Natural Awakenings, March 31, 2015,
https://www.naturalawakenings.com/2015/03/31/274262/
strong-winds-strong-roots-what-trees-teach-us-about-life.

Day 7: Roller Coaster

1. "Your Emotions and Cancer," Canadian Cancer Society, https://
www.cancer.ca/en/cancer-information/living-with-cancer/your-
emotions-and-cancer/?region=on.
2. National Cancer Institute, https://www.cancer.gov/about-cancer/
coping/feelings, "Feelings and Cancer."
3. Nancy P. Morgan, Kristi D. Graves, Elizabeth A. Poggi, and Bruce
D. Cheson, "Implementing an Expressive Writing Study in a Cancer Clinic," *The Oncologist* 13, no. 2 (2008): 196–204.
4. Ibid.
5. American Cancer Society, https://www.cancer.org/treatment/
treatments-and-side-effects/emotional-side-effects/distress/coping-
tips.html, "How can I help myself cope with cancer?"

Day 9: Lonely

1. Barbara Tako, "Cancer Is Lonely Enough, Don't Do Cancer Alone,"
CURE, March 7, 2016, https://www.curetoday.com/community/
barbara-tako/2016/03/cancer-is-lonely-enough-dont-do-cancer-
alone.
2. Lisa Masters, "The Loneliness of Cancer," HuffPost, May 6, 2014,
https://www.huffpost.com/entry/the-loneliness-of-cancer_b_
4913580.
3. "Your Emotions and Cancer," Canadian Cancer Society, https://
www.cancer.ca/en/cancer-information/living-with-cancer/your-
emotions-and-cancer/?
4. Luke 22:44–45 AMPC.
5. John 18:3 AMP.
6. Matthew 28:20 AMP.

Day 10: Support

1. Charles Stanley, comment on Romans 12:15, in *The Charles F. Stanley Life Principles Bible* (Nashville: Thomas Nelson, 2005), 1325.

Day 11: Promoters and Protectors

1. Margaret Feinberg, quoted in Jonathan Merritt, "Christian Author Breaks Silence, Shares Horrors of Breast Cancer Battle," Religion News Service, January 14, 2015, https://religionnews.com/2015/01/14/christian-author-breaks-silence-shares-horrors-breast-cancer-battle/.

Day 12: Anger

1. David B. Feldman, "Why the Five Stages of Grief Are Wrong," Psychology Today, July 7, 2017, https://www.psychologytoday.com/us/blog/supersurvivors/201707/why-the-five-stages-grief-are-wrong.

Day 13: The Cancer Chapter

1. The Online Etymology Dictionary, s.v. "author (n.)," https://www.etymonline.com/search?q=author.
2. Hebrews 5:9 KJV.
3. Hebrews 12:2 KJV.

Day 14: Sar-Shalom

1. Skip Moen, "Prince of Peace," SkipMoen.com, December, 21, 2009, https://www.skipmoen.com/2009/12/prince-of-peace/; Cambridge Bible for Schools and Colleges, Isaiah 6:9, Bible Hub, https://biblehub.com/commentaries/isaiah/9-6.htm.
2. Moen, "Prince of Peace."
3. John 14:27.
4. Galatians 5:22–23 NIV.

Day 16: Sing!

1. Tom Olson, "Seven Biblical Reasons Why Singing Matters," Unlocking the Bible, September 21, 2017, https://unlockingthebible.org/2017/09/seven-biblical-reasons-why-singing-matters/.
2. Second Chronicles 20:21–22 NIV.
3. Steven J. Cole, "Psalms an Overview: God's Inspired Handbook," April 18, 2013, https://bible.org/seriespage/psalms-overview-god's-inspired-hymnbook.

Day 17: Brain Fog

1. Editorial Team, "Brain Fog as a Treatment Side Effect," Prostrate Cancer.net, August 24, 2018, https://prostatecancer.net/living/brain-fog-treatment-side-effect/.
2. Editorial Team, "Get Talking: Side Effect Frustrations," Prostrate Cancer.net, January 18, 2019, https://prostatecancer.net/living/side-effect-frustrations/.

Day 18: Jehovah-Rapha

1. Robert Murray McCheyne, "Fourth Pastoral Letter," Edinburgh, February 20, 1839, in *The Life and Remains: Letters, Lectures and Poems of the Rev. Robert Murray Mccheyne, Minister of St. Peter's Church, Dundee*, 6th ed., ed. Andrew A. Bonar (New York: Robert Carter, 1848), 168.

Day 19: New Clothes

1. Michael J. Easley, "The Constant Distraction: Living with Chronic Pain," in *Beyond Suffering Bible* (Carol Stream, IL: Tyndale, 2016), 1489.
2. Martin Luther's Bible Commentary, Galatians 3:26, https://www.biblestudytools.com/commentaries/luther/galatians/3.html.

Day 20: Prayer

1. "Deep Inspiratory Breath-Hold," Northwestern Medicine, https://www.nm.org/conditions-and-care-areas/treatments/deep-inspiratory-breath-hold.

Day 21: Look Up

1. Lauren Daigle, "Lauren Daigle - About The Album: Look Up Child," YouTube video, March 22, 2019, https://www.youtube.com/watch?v=h-10AaKKUsI.
2. D. L. Moody, quoted in Joseph Fort Newton, *River of Years* (New York: Lippincott, 1946), 312.

Day 22: Overwhelmed

1. Charles Spurgeon, *Morning & Evening* (Peabody, MA: Hendrickson Publishers Marketing, LLC, 1997), 286.

Day 23: Gorgeous

1. "Body Image," Livestrong, https://www.livestrong.org/we-can-help/emotional-and-physical-effects-of-treatment/body-image.

2. Jessica T. DeFrank, Christian Mehta, Kevin D. Stein, and Frank Baker, "Body Image Dissatisfaction in Cancer Survivors," *Oncology Nursing Forum* 34, no. 3 (2007): E36–41.
3. "Body Image," Livestrong.
4. Matthew Henry, commentary on 1 Samuel 16, Blue Letter Bible, https://www.blueletterbible.org/Comm/mhc/1Sa/1Sa_016.cfm.
5. Timothy Keller, *Walking with God through Pain and Suffering* (New York: Penguin Group, 2013), 181.

Day 24: Jonathan and Jehoshaphat
1. Ocular Melanoma Foundation, http://www.ocularmelanoma.org.

Day 25: The Hardest Part
1. James 4:6 AMPC.

Day 26: Rebel Cells
1. First Corinthians 12:12.
2. First Corinthians 12:16–18.
3. Galatians 5:13 AMP.
4. Richard Beliveau and Denis Gingras, *Foods to Fight Cancer* (New York: DK, 2017), 31.
5. Ibid., 28.

Day 28: Fear Not
1. Charles Stanley, "What the Bible Says about How Adversity Reveals Our Level of Faith," in *The Charles F. Stanley Life Principles Bible* (Nashville: Thomas Nelson, 2005), 1163.
2. Bill Gaultiere, "Fear Not . . . 365 Days a Year," Christian Broadcasting Network, October 21, 2011, https://www1.cbn.com/soul transformation/archive/2011/10/21/fear-not.-365-days-a-year.
3. Katherine Weber, "Rick Warren: Why God Encourages Christians to 'Fear Not' 365 Times in the Bible," *The Christian Post*, April 30, 2016, https://www.christianpost.com/news/rick-warren-why-god-encourages-christians-to-fear-not-365-times-in-the-bible.html.
4. Jerry White, "Meditation: Learning to Think of God," *Decision*, June 24, 2015, https://decisionmagazine.com/meditation-learning-to-think-of-god/.

Day 29: Hope
1. First Corinthians 13:13.

2. "Your Emotions and Cancer," Canadian Cancer Society, https://www.cancer.ca/en/cancer-information/living-with-cancer/your-emotions-and-cancer/?region=on.

3. Mark Batterson, *In a Pit with a Lion on a Snowy Day: How to Survive and Thrive When Opportunity Roars* (New York: Multnomah, 2016), 79.

Day 30: What's Next?

1. Sheila M. Chibnall-Treptow, in *Pink Prayer Book: Coping, Healing, Surviving, Thriving*, ed. Diana Losciale (Liguori, MO: Liguori Publications, 2008), 21.

2. John Piper, *Don't Waste Your Cancer* (Wheaton, IL: Crossway, 2011). Free download or paperback, kindle, or audiobook purchase from https://www.desiringgod.org/books/dont-waste-your-cancer.

About the Author

Deborah Barr is a versatile writer and speaker with special interests in health and wellness topics, Alzheimer's disease, dementia caregiving, and Christian growth. She is a master certified health education specialist (MCHES®) with a bachelor's degree in journalism and a master's degree in health education. *Strength for the Cancer Journey* is her sixth book. You can read more about Debbie at https://www.debbiebarr.com, linkedin.com/in/debbiebarr, and amazon.com/author/debbiebarr.

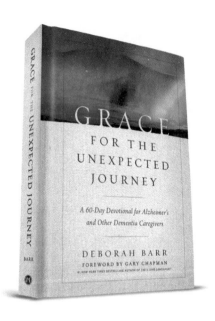

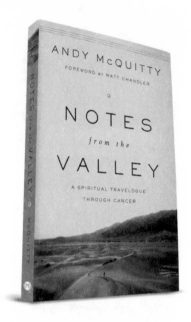

A MEMOIR OF CANCER

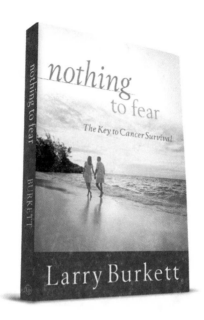

MOODY
Publishers®

*From the Word **to** Life®*

Larry Burkett tells his personal journey of a seven-year battle with cancer. Filled with intimate stories and wisdom from the Word, this book will be a great help to the thousands of people who fight this disease. Larry's legacy continues today, and his words still bring hope to those in need of encouragement.

978-0-8024-1434-2 | also available as an eBook

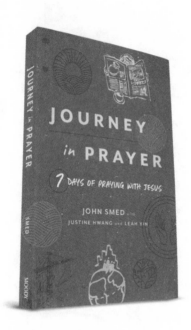